PRAYING
the
GOSPELS

WITH
FR. MITCH PACWA, SJ

PRAYING
the
GOSPELS

WITH
FR. MITCH PACWA, SJ

Jesus Launches His Ministry

Published by The Word Among Us Press
7115 Guilford Drive, Suite 100
Frederick, Maryland 21704
www.wau.org

19 18 17 16 15   1 2 3 4 5

Imprimi potest: V. Rev. Brian G. Paulson, SJ
            Chicago-Detroit Province of the Society of Jesus
            March 20, 2015

ISBN: 978-1-59325-268-7
eISBN: 978-1-59325-269-8

Cover design by Koechel Peterson & Associates
Cover icon of the Wedding at Cana © Monastery Icons
Used with permission.

Made and printed in the United States of America

Library of Congress Control Number: 2015934606

Contents

Foreword

During my years as Bishop of Fort Worth, I was blessed to be able to come to know Fr. Mitch Pacwa personally through our ministry at Our Lady of Lebanon in Lewisville, Texas, during Holy Week. Particularly on Holy Thursday, Fr. Pacwa and I would assist our good friend Fr. Asaad with confessions on Holy Thursday into the wee hours of the morning. It was a blessed time of the Triduum for all of us!

These days in the Diocese of Orange, we have been spending a lot of time and reflection on "intentional discipleship," meaning that all we do and seek to do flows from a personal encounter with the Lord and a personal relationship with him. This is no "program" but a way of life.

Fr. Pacwa's book *Jesus Launches His Ministry*, as a part of the series *Praying the Gospels with Fr. Mitch Pacwa, SJ*, certainly calls us to do just that: have an encounter with the living Lord so that we are disciples first before all else! To illustrate this point precisely, I turn to the conclusion of the second meditation: "Ask Jesus for the grace to humbly integrate all that we have been and all that we are into all that he wants us to be in the future. Speak as a friend to a Friend who is able to include each of us, with our real background and actual personality, into his mission to invite all people into the kingdom of God" (page 20).

I believe this book will help me, and all of us, have that conversation with the Lord, hear his voice clearly, and follow him!

Most Rev. Kevin W. Vann, JCD, DD
Bishop of Orange, California

Introduction

My earlier book, *How to Listen When God Is Speaking*, outlined some basic principles underlying our life of prayer and some ways of how to pray. This book builds upon that one by presenting the life of Jesus Christ as a source for the content of meditation. The style is modeled on that recommended by St. Ignatius Loyola in his Spiritual Exercises.

However, this book is not a presentation of the four weeks of the Spiritual Exercises as he intended them. Rather, it is a series of meditations on various events in the public life of Christ, such as one might choose to consider in the Second Week of the Spiritual Exercises. The goal in this book is to spend more time on specific events in the life of Christ so that we can get to know him better.

Because we need to savor the Gospel texts, I have purposely limited the number of verses in each meditation. Each chapter deals with a specific Gospel event, and each event is broken into short passages that are the subject of the meditation. Sometimes I use the same verse for more than one meditation in order to reflect on all its implications. I have chosen to focus in this book on the beginning of Jesus' ministry, and I will continue in a second book to offer meditations on Jesus' time in Galilee.

After the verses are a few paragraphs describing some of the background of the text—from the geography and scenery to the Jewish customs and ideas that lie behind the event. These are meant to help situate the events of Jesus' life and aid the imagination in entering the scenes. Jesus lived in a Middle Eastern society of two thousand years ago. The customs and language may be strange to modern people, so it is useful to try to understand these ancient ways of life and thought. However, the other goal is to see that through these cultural differences shines the humanity common to us all. The specific words and customs may differ from the modern world's ideas and expressions, but we can discover connections with the deeper truths of humanity once we better understand the context. This may help us relate our own experiences to those of the people in these stories and then discover important elements about our own relationship with Jesus Christ.

More than simply discovering Jesus' personality, we can also seek to understand his vision for the world, for salvation, and for us today. Many of the comments on the texts and the questions for meditation are rooted in Jesus' own mission to the world and his summons to his very human disciples to come, follow him, and take up his mission. However, the goal is not for this book to challenge you, but for you to bring these questions to your prayerful conversation with Jesus so that *he* can challenge you. Letting the reader's relationship with Jesus deepen and develop is my top priority.

May the Lord Holy Spirit guide your prayer and direct you to Jesus Christ, so that with him, you may give glory to the heavenly Father.

Fr. Mitch Pacwa, SJ

CHAPTER 1

The Baptism of Jesus

MATTHEW 3:1-17

John the Baptist and Jesus

In those days came John the Baptist, preaching in the wilderness of Judea, "Repent, for the kingdom of heaven is at hand." For this is he who was spoken of by the prophet Isaiah when he said,

"The voice of one crying in the wilderness:

Prepare the way of the Lord,

make his paths straight."

Now John wore a garment of camel's hair, and a leather girdle around his waist; and his food was locusts and wild honey. Then went out to him Jerusalem and all Judea and all the region about the Jordan, and they were baptized by him in the river Jordan, confessing their sins.

But when he saw many of the Pharisees and Sadducees coming for baptism, he said to them, "You brood of vipers! Who warned you to flee from the wrath to come? Bear fruit that befits repentance, and do not presume to say to yourselves, 'We have Abraham as our father'; for I tell you, God is able from these stones to raise up children to Abraham. Even now the axe is laid to the root of the trees; every tree therefore that does not bear good fruit is cut down and thrown into the fire.

"I baptize you with water for repentance, but he who is coming after me is mightier than I, whose sandals I am not worthy to carry; he will baptize you with the Holy Spirit and with fire. His winnowing fork is in his hand, and he will clear his threshing floor and gather his wheat into the granary, but the chaff he will burn with unquenchable fire." (Matthew 3:1-12)

Consider Matthew 3:1-12 and the way in which John the Baptist was clearly in control of events and words. He boldly spoke the message that would be Christ's: "Repent, for the kingdom of heaven is at hand" (3:2). He identified the Pharisees and Sadducees as "You brood of vipers!" (3:7) and ordered them, "Bear fruit that befits repentance" (3:8). He warned of a coming judgment against all who choose any form of evil: "The axe is laid to the root of the trees; every tree therefore that does not bear good fruit is cut down and thrown into the fire" (3:10).

In contrast to his bold, strong stance against any opponent of God's righteousness, John highlighted his smallness with the greatness of the One whose coming he announced: "I baptize you with water for repentance, but he who is coming after me is mightier than I, whose sandals I am not worthy to carry; he will baptize you with the Holy Spirit and with fire" (Matthew 3:11). This is the One who would judge all people, like a farmer who separates wheat and chaff: he will "gather his wheat into the granary, but the chaff he will burn with unquenchable fire" (3:12).

John asserted Jesus' superiority over himself and his ministry when his own disciples told him, "Rabbi, he who was with you beyond the Jordan, to whom you bore witness, here he is, baptizing, and all are going to him" (John 3:26). John displayed no jealousy at all because he recognized one of the most basic principles of the spiritual life: "No one can receive anything except what is given him from heaven" (3:27).

Consider two points in regard to John the Baptist. First, he realized that God himself is the source of all the gifts and charisms that a person possesses. The issue at hand is not the fame, the adulation, the size of the following, or any other benefit that might accrue to the person who has been gifted by God.

In what ways do we hold the mentality of John's disciples, who feared that Jesus was becoming more popular than their own teacher? Do we think like John's disciples, who were centered on maintaining their egos through success, or do we center on God and the accomplishment of his will by our faithful and generous use of the gifts he has given us? If we turn our attention to the gifts, their effects or, most dangerous, their benefits to us, we place our spiritual lives in jeopardy. God must always be recognized as the source of all our good and the goal of our small accomplishments for his glory.

Second, do we have John's attitude toward Jesus Christ? Do we recognize not only that he is "mightier than I" but also see our own smallness and unworthiness to even "carry his sandals"? We are often tempted to emphasize the importance of our contributions to the service of God and the Church. Yet what is that compared to Jesus' authority and power to "baptize you with the Holy Spirit and with fire" (Matthew 3:11)? Jesus can pour out the infinite Person of the Holy Spirit upon us; we can receive only a small portion of that gift. Jesus can test us with fire, while we can only hope that we pass the test. Let us take to heart the truth that John the Baptist spoke so clearly:

> "I said, I am not the Christ, but I have been sent before him. He who has the bride is the bridegroom; the friend of the bridegroom, who stands and hears him, rejoices greatly at the bridegroom's voice; therefore this joy of mine is now full. He must increase, but I must decrease." (John 3:28-30)

Conclude with an Our Father.

_____

_____

_____

_____

_____

_____

_____

_____

_____

_____

_____

_____

_____

_____

_____

_____

_____

_____

Jesus' Journey to the Jordan

Then Jesus came from Galilee to the Jordan to John,
to be baptized by him. (Matthew 3:13)

After the return of the Holy Family from Egypt, St. Matthew says that Jesus remained in Nazareth in Galilee (2:22-23). Matthew's silence about Jesus' twenty-some years in Nazareth puzzles some readers, who try to fill in the gaps with quite divergent stories about the miracles he performed as a young boy.

Whether these stories come from the Infancy Gospels of the fourth and fifth centuries, or from people who claim to receive knowledge through visions, locutions, or other messages (which do not corroborate each other), it is better to remain with the silence. The Church accepts the ordinary quality of Jesus' life in Nazareth as one of family relationships and common labor and has rejected the acceptance of stories about fabulous miracles, such as the young Jesus making clay pigeons and breathing into them to make them come alive. The modern stories about Jesus traveling to Egypt, India, Tibet, and elsewhere to learn the magical powers that were the source of his miracles are also strongly rejected. The first type of story emphasizes the power of his divinity; the second suggests that he is a man whose power came from other human sources. The Church simply accepts that when God became flesh, he was truly human and divine, with the ordinary life of human family and human labor serving as a model for the ordinariness that most people live.

But it is ordinariness that many people want to avoid at all costs. Perhaps we imagine ourselves acquiring money or fame, thinking that it will make our lives better. We might lament that our lives are boring and blame our circumstances—parents who did not give us enough, or schools or jobs that did not recognize our natural talents and abilities. Some adopt unusual clothing or hair coloring or styles so that they won't look like everyone else. And in sometimes desperate attempts to get noticed, people record embarrassing, shameful, and even pain-filled events on the Internet.

Archbishop Fulton J. Sheen said that Jesus spent thirty years obeying human parents, three years teaching disciples, and three hours redeeming the world. For most of his life, the Son of God obeyed two holy parents, learned his foster father's trade, and became known as the carpenter in Nazareth (Luke 2:51—"He went down with them and came to Nazareth, and was obedient to them.") As we consider this aspect of Jesus as he leaves home to begin his public ministry, we can ask for the grace to accept our lives—both our lives now and as we grew up—more humbly. Can we turn from the temptation to complain about the routineness and boredom of everyday life? Can we turn from the temptation to pursue pride through self-exposure or in other ways that draw attention to ourselves?

Consider Jesus walking down the high hill from Nazareth to the very broad and long fertile Jezreel Valley. Think about him journeying along the Jordan River Valley to Jericho and his arrival at the place where John was baptizing. Picture yourself walking this seventy-five-mile journey with him, and ask him what his life was like in Nazareth. How might he describe his blessed mother, Mary, St. Joseph, his memories of growing up in their home, and the selfless love they each showed him?

What would he say about the trade St. Joseph taught him and the labor he did for his neighbors? How did the love of his family shape his way of thinking about human beings and the needs he would address during his public ministry?

Next, consider what you might share with Jesus about your family. Describe to him the love of your mother, father, brothers, sisters, and other family members. What pleasant memories do you have? What areas in your family of origin might have been broken? Were there internal arguments and fights, absence of parents because of too much work, or addictions that held them back from being loving? Was there divorce? Were your parents ever married in the first place? Did you experience abuse of any kind, and if so, did it evoke great pain, anger, or resentment?

We can also discuss with Jesus our own temptations to pride, our rebellion against our parents' legitimate requests and demands, our failures to develop the gifts we have because we wanted some other, often far-fetched dream. What would Jesus say to us about each aspect of our lives that we tell him? Let this conversation help you view every aspect of your life in the truth of who you really are as you walk through Galilee to Judea with the One who is Truth personified.

Ask Jesus for the grace to humbly integrate all that we have been and all that we are into all that he wants us to be in the future. Speak as a friend to a Friend who is able to include each of us, with our real background and actual personality, into his mission to invite all people into the kingdom of God. Consider this exercise later as Jesus calls his early disciples, corrects their behavior, and fashions them into his apostles.

Conclude with an Our Father.

_____

_____

_____

_____

_____

_____

_____

_____

_____

_____

_____

_____

_____

_____

_____

_____

_____

_____

_____

_____

_____

John's Confusion

"I need to be baptized by you, and do you come to me?"
(Matthew 3:14)

This verse invites us into John's confusion during his encounter with Jesus at the Jordan. Quite humbly, John recognizes the greater One standing before him, and he wants to submit to Jesus' superior baptism "with the Holy Spirit and with fire" (Matthew 3:11). However, Jesus has come to be baptized by John, and this humility is beyond John's comprehension.

As with so many other people in the Gospels, John does not understand Jesus' request because he does not fully understand the heavenly Father's will. Recall that St. Joseph did not immediately understand the Virgin Mary's pregnancy; the Blessed Mother did not understand why Jesus had remained in the Temple for three days; and now neither does John understand why Jesus would ask John to baptize him. Even to the holiest persons with major roles in Christ's mission to redeem the world, Jesus is a mystery who transcends their understanding of the steps toward fulfilling that mission.

If even John the Baptist, St. Joseph, and the Blessed Virgin Mary did not see how Jesus' actions fit into their understanding of God's plan, should we be surprised when we fail to grasp God's plan for us as it unfolds step-by-step? Think about those times in our lives when we try to find God's will for us, obey him, and be faithful to his word and teaching. Consider, for example, choosing a spouse or a religious vocation, or looking for a job that best uses our skills, provides for our family, and serves God. Consider those times when our well-intentioned ideas and plans seem so perfect but then go awry. Do we not wonder why God let the wrong turn of events happen? Do we not ask God, "If I am trying to do your will, why don't my ideas work out as planned?" Rarely do we have clarity about God's will for us in those moments; often we wonder, sometimes we are confused, and when a great idea goes wrong, we can even become angry at the situation and at God.

Yet, if you are old enough, consider in retrospect what may have happened. Sometimes a seeming mistake or false turn gets changed into something far better and more worthwhile than the natural projection of our original plan. Were you able to come to the point of seeing yourself in St. Paul's words: "We know that in everything God works for good with those who love him, who are called according to his purpose" (Romans 8:28)?

Sometimes, like St. Joseph and St. John the Baptist, who both died before the mystery of Jesus' life was completed, we might only know God's plan from a heavenly perspective. Then we are called to trust that we will see the whole picture from the perspective of eternity.

Reflect on your life and those turning points that were beyond your control. Did you come to see God's plan start to unfold? Do you trust in God's providence, with all of its mysteriousness? Talk to Jesus as a friend to a Friend about how you can grow in trust.

Conclude with an Our Father.

_____

_____

_____

_____

_____

_____

_____

_____

_____

_____

_____

_____

_____

_____

_____

_____

_____

_____

_____

_____

_____

_____

_____

MEDITATION 4

Fulfilling All Righteousness

But Jesus answered him, "Let it be so now; for thus it is fitting for us
to fulfill all righteousness." (Matthew 3:15)

Consider Jesus' response to John's deference: being baptized is the proper way to fulfill "all righteousness."
Clearly, John recognized Jesus as the One who could baptize him "with the Holy Spirit and with fire" (Matthew 3:11),
and he desired it. However, for "now," Jesus needed to receive
John's baptism because "all righteousness" was not yet fulfilled.
What does that mean?

Consider that Jesus understands his whole mission as one
of "fulfillment" on a variety of levels. First, in ways unique to
him, he fulfills the prophecies of the Old Testament: his birth
from a virgin—Matthew 1:22-23; his return from Egypt—2:15;
his healing of human sickness—8:17; his being a gentle Messiah—12:17-19; his teaching in parables—13:34-35; his ride
into Jerusalem on a donkey—21:4-5. For that reason, he taught,
"Think not that I have come to abolish the law and the prophets; I have come not to abolish them but to fulfill them" (5:17).

Second, he came to fulfill the Father's will, as he frequently
stated:

"My food is to do the will of him who sent me, and to accomplish his work." (John 4:34)

"I have come down from heaven, not to do my own will, but the
will of him who sent me." (John 6:38)

"I seek not my own will but the will of him who sent me."
(John 5:30)

"My Father, if it be possible, let this cup pass from me; nevertheless, not as I will, but as thou wilt." (Matthew 26:39)

Jesus' mission to fulfill all righteousness will include both the fulfillment of the Old Testament prophecies and the Father's will, since the prophecies express that will.

Third, as Jesus will later predict and fulfill in action, he had to suffer, die, and rise again in order to redeem the world. Certainly his suffering, death, and resurrection were also the fulfillment of Old Testament prophecies and of the Father's will, as Jesus explained to the disciples on the road to Emmaus and to the disciples in the upper room on the day of his resurrection (Luke 24:25-26, 44). Yet at the same time, the three days of suffering, dying, burial, and resurrection were the fulfillment of the Father's will that gave power to all that Jesus would bequeath to the world, and precisely in this did he fulfill all righteousness. The sacraments, including baptism, would be effective only because the righteousness Jesus fulfilled in his death and resurrection would be its power. Recall St. Paul's teaching that baptism draws the redeemed into the mystery of Christ's death so that we might rise with him:

Do you not know that all of us who have been baptized into Christ Jesus were baptized into his death? We were buried therefore with him by baptism into death, so that as Christ was raised from the dead by the glory of the Father, we too might walk in newness of life. For if we have been united with him in a death like his, we shall certainly be united with him in a resurrection like his. We know that our old self was crucified with him so that the sinful body might be destroyed, and we might no longer be enslaved to sin. (Romans 6:3-6)

Though John the Baptist desired Jesus' superior baptism, it was not yet time to give it, since its superior power would derive from Jesus' death and resurrection, which would take place after John's own martyrdom, a fact he could not yet perceive.

How well do you perceive the power of your own baptism? When you bring your children to be baptized, is it more of an opportunity to gather the family for a celebration, or do you think about what Jesus is about to effect within that child? Do you give pause to consider the drama of Jesus' death and resurrection taking place within the soul of your child and the indelible character being stamped for all eternity by the Holy Spirit to mark the child as a citizen of heaven?

Do you know the anniversary of your own baptism? Ask the parish staff at the church where you were baptized for the date, and try to imagine that day. Most important, seek to understand the Scripture verse "Baptism . . . now saves you" (1 Peter 3:21). Consider that the fulfillment of all righteousness occurred within your soul and began the process of forgiving sin, starting with original sin, and, if you were baptized at a later stage of life, any other sins you may have committed.

Examine your conscience about the ways in which you cooperate with all the righteousness that Jesus has won for you. Ask yourself these questions: How well do I cooperate with the graces of my baptism to avoid further sin? Do I live in this world as one who considers my citizenship in heaven as more important than the values and concerns of this world? Do I "seek first his kingdom and his righteousness," as Jesus commands (Matthew 6:33)?

Conclude with an Our Father.

_____

_____

_____

_____

_____

_____

_____

_____

_____

_____

_____

_____

_____

_____

_____

_____

_____

_____

_____

Jesus Is Baptized

And . . . Jesus was baptized. (Matthew 3:16)

People had come to John and "were baptized by him in the river Jordan, confessing their sins" (Matthew 3:6). Pharisees and Sadducees had come to John to judge whether he was a prophet, and he judged their evil deeds (3:7-10). Jesus entered the water neither confessing sin nor being judged by John but simply being baptized. Why did Jesus accept John's baptism? After all, he "committed no sin; no guile was found on his lips" (1 Peter 2:22, citing Isaiah 53:9; see also 2 Corinthians 5:21; 1 John 3:5; and Hebrews 4:15; 7:26)

Scripture offers an answer to this question: Jesus humbles himself in order to identify with us sinners so that we can better understand him and meet him. In Hebrews we read, "For we have not a high priest who is unable to sympathize with our weaknesses, but one who in every respect has been tempted as we are, yet without sinning" (4:15).

If that were not the case, we would be so overwhelmed by Christ's display of holiness that we would say with Simon Peter, in reaction to the miraculous catch of fish, "Depart from me, for I am a sinful man, O Lord" (Luke 5:8). However, Jesus did not become flesh in order to frighten sinners away but to draw them to himself. For that reason, he stands with the sinners on Jordan's bank and is baptized by John as they were.

Consider how St. Paul, who understood himself to be "the foremost of sinners" (1 Timothy 1:15), recognized that Jesus Christ, "though he was in the form of God, did not count equality with God a thing to be grasped, but emptied himself, taking the form of a servant, being born in the likeness of men" (Philippians 2:6-7). This may help us to understand why Jesus starts the public ministry with a baptism by which he identifies with sinners yet without becoming a sinner to do so.

Imagine yourself as one of the people coming to confess your sins and be baptized by John. Consider the actual sins you have committed throughout your life, including those committed since your own baptism. With your personal sins in mind, hear John summon you and the others to repent; also hear him address the Pharisees and Sadducees as a "brood of vipers" (Matthew 3:7; Luke 3:7). Jesus is asked to baptize John. Still, Jesus enters the waters, just like you. Jesus meets you as you seek the forgiveness of your sins in the Jordan River. What would you say to him as he meets you there? What would he say to you about your life as he stands in the waters of baptism with you?

Conclude with an Our Father.

_____

_____

_____

_____

_____

_____

_____

_____

_____

_____

The Manifestation of the Blessed Trinity

And when Jesus was baptized, he went up immediately from the water, and behold, the heavens were opened and he saw the Spirit of God descending like a dove, and alighting on him; and lo, a voice from heaven, saying, "This is my beloved Son, with whom I am well pleased." (Matthew 3:16-17)

When Jesus comes out of the Jordan River, "the heavens were opened," a passive event indicating that the Lord God was actively opening them to reveal something important. From Abraham forward, the people of Israel learned—often through painful punishment and even exile to Babylon—that the Lord is the one and only God; there is no other (Isaiah 45:5, 14, 18, 21-22; 46:9). Now, as Jesus emerges from the water of the Jordan, the one God reveals that he is a unity of three Persons—a Trinity. The Father speaks to identify Jesus as his Son, and the Holy Spirit hovers over him as the Spirit had done at the creation of the world (Genesis 1:2).

Jesus had not informed John that a great manifestation of God would occur over him. He is no more seeking to demonstrate his power or importance before John than he would when the devil tempted him to jump off the Temple (Matthew 4:6). Rather, as Jesus fulfills "all righteousness" (3:15), a new level of the knowledge of God results from his humble obedience.

When the voice from heaven announces that Jesus is his "beloved Son" (Matthew 3:17), the speaker indicates that he is the Father of Jesus. None of the prophets or teachers in Israel had made such a claim regarding their personal relationship with God; instead, the prophets spoke of God as Israel's father in a national sense. Israel is identified as the Lord's son (Exodus 4:22 and Hosea 11:1); Israel is criticized for failing to accept God as Father (Deuteronomy 32:6, Jeremiah 3:19, and Malachi 1:6); God is said to be a father to the people of Israel (Jeremiah 31:9, Malachi 2:10; Isaiah 63:16, 64:8). In contrast, when Jesus exits the water of baptism, the Father acknowledges Jesus as his Son, as he will do again at the Transfiguration (Matthew 17:5; Mark 9:7; Luke 9:35).

In addition to identifying Jesus as his Son, the Father changes these prophetic words of Isaiah: "Behold my servant, whom I uphold, / my chosen, in whom my soul delights; / I have put my Spirit upon him, / he will bring forth justice to the nations" (42:1). While this verse shows that Jesus is fulfilling the prophecy, the Father is changing the term from "servant" to "Son." By quoting this prophecy, the Father thereby indicates its fulfillment.

Imagine the descent of the Holy Spirit upon the newly baptized Jesus, resting upon him like a dove. Clearly, the Holy Spirit gently descends and the Father speaks of his pleasure with his Son in order to pour out his infinite love upon him. The Father and the Holy Spirit are affirming pleasure at the first stage of the Son's mission—the thirty years of quiet family life with Mary and Joseph—but they are also blessing this new turning point of Jesus' public ministry, as well as reassuring Jesus before his long fast and the devil's temptations.

We sinners who receive baptism become adopted sons and daughters of God. Picture the Blessed Trinity showing delight over you. Imagine the Father saying to you, "My beloved child, with whom I am well pleased." With faith, know that the Father speaks such words to you. Are you tempted to think, "If God takes such delight in me, then why is my life so hard? Why have so many things gone badly?" Precisely with that thought in mind, consider all that is in store for Jesus as he is led by the Holy Spirit to fast for forty days and be strongly tempted by the devil. Consider how many people will come to reject and hate him, to the point of plotting to kill him. Recall his suffering and crucifixion, during which he will pray, "Father, into thy hands I commit my spirit" (Luke 23:46).

Can you remember moments when you felt a peace that seemed to overwhelm you with God's loving presence? Can you recall even a brief moment in which you felt a sense of security beyond anything the world or its people can offer? Consider such moments as the Father speaks to you as he spoke to Jesus: "Behold my child, in whom I am well pleased."

Speak to the Father about the meaning of the pleasure he takes in you. Receive his loving approval as the primary consolation throughout all of life, especially through its painfully difficult moments. Ask him to help you accept these consolations as your source of strength in moving ahead on the mission he gives you in life, and follow where the Holy Spirit leads you, as Jesus did.

Conclude with an Our Father.

_____

_____

_____

_____

_____

_____

_____

_____

_____

_____

_____

_____

_____

_____

_____

_____

_____

_____

_____

_____

_____

_____

_____

_____

_____

_____

_____

_____

_____

_____

_____

CHAPTER 2

Temptations in the Wilderness

MATTHEW 4:1-11

MEDITATION 1

The Wilderness

*Then Jesus was led up by the Spirit into the wilderness
to be tempted by the devil. (Matthew 4:1)*

The shores of the Jordan River are lush with reeds and other vegetation, but the dry desert wilderness begins a very short distance from the river. Very little rain falls in that region, since the warm and often hot air of the Jordan River Valley, which is about thirteen hundred feet below sea level, dissipates the rain clouds as they pass over the Mount of Olives twenty miles to the west. Apart from the Jericho oasis, very little can grow in that rocky desert. The water of the Jordan comes from the melting snow on Mount Hermon, on the border with Lebanon. Israel completed its forty-year desert wandering just east of the river, while the dry wilderness is the site of Jesus' forty-day fast and temptation.

We would do well to consider the fact that this same wilderness in which Jesus experienced the temptations of Satan was also the wilderness in which the people of Israel had experienced their own temptations. The Israelites escaped Pharaoh's last attempt to destroy them when they walked dry-shod through the sea and the sea closed in upon the pursuing Egyptian army (Exodus 14:21-31). However, only three days after their songs of exultation celebrating the Lord's mighty redemption through the waters of the sea (15:1-21), they grumbled against Moses because the water was too bitter to drink. The Lord saved them and sweetened the water and led them to an oasis (15:22-27). In the next month, they ran out of food and grumbled that it would have been better to stay in Egypt and die there. The Lord sent them manna for the rest of their desert wandering (Exodus 16). Again they grumbled, this time for water after they left the oasis, so Moses struck the rock that poured out water (17:1-7). While Moses was on Mount Sinai receiving instructions on how to build the ark of the covenant and the tabernacle, the people grumbled and induced Aaron to make the golden calf (Exodus 32).

When the people left Sinai, they complained that they were tired of manna from heaven and wanted meat and vegetables (Numbers 11). Just before they were led into the Promised Land to conquer the various nations, they rebelled because they were afraid, so God made them wander another forty years (Numbers 14). Yet again the people complained about a lack of water and about their disgust with eating manna, so the Lord punished them with a plague of serpents (21:4-9). Again the people complained that they wished they were in Egypt because they longed for the foods they had eaten there. Then the Lord told Moses to speak to the rock to make water come out, but he disobeyed and struck it twice with his staff, and so Moses was not permitted to lead his people into the Promised Land (20:2-13). Finally, the men committed adultery and fornication with Moabite women, who induced them to worship Baal (Numbers 25).

Consider these occasions in which Israel grumbled and complained against Moses and the Lord because of food and water. Then consider the people's failure to keep the first commandment to worship only the Lord God, instead worshipping the golden calf (Exodus 32) and Baal (Numbers 25). Look at their failure to take the kingdoms offered them because they were afraid to trust that the Lord could lead them to victory against the petty kingdoms of Canaan, though he had saved them from

Egypt, the greatest superpower of the age. Repeatedly, they failed to withstand temptations.

Now look at your own life history. In what ways are you repeatedly tempted? Are there bad habits that have become very difficult to overcome? Are there areas in which, through ignorance and inexperience, you fail to understand or obey God's law and truth? Have you found that some areas of giving in to temptation lead you into further sin? Do you sometimes feel that you have already sinned, so you might as well keep on doing it? Do you sometimes think, "Everyone I know is doing this, so it must be okay"?

Consider how these temptations are your own experience of being like ancient Israel, wandering in a moral desert in which a virtuous life eludes you as it did them. Speak with Jesus about the difficulties you have in overcoming temptation and in practicing virtue.

Conclude with the publican's prayer: "God, be merciful to me a sinner" (Luke 18:13).

_____

_____

_____

_____

_____

_____

_____

_____

....

Led by the Spirit

Then Jesus was led up by the Spirit into the wilderness to be tempted by the devil. (Matthew 4:1)

Many Christians find it very odd that the very Holy Spirit who hovered over Jesus at his baptism would be the One to lead him into the wilderness in order to be tempted. Why would the Holy Spirit lead him into temptation? Does this mean that God the Holy Spirit is tempting God the Son? Does that mean that God tempts us too?

Scripture answers the last question very explicitly: "Let no one say when he is tempted, 'I am tempted by God'; for God cannot be tempted with evil and he himself tempts no one" (James 1:13). If God cannot tempt us, then what does it mean that the Holy Spirit led Jesus to be tempted by the devil?

Perhaps this image may help. Military generals train and equip soldiers for war, but they do not want their soldiers to be injured or die. At the same time, their training is not to make a career by living on a military post or by walking on the parade ground. Rather, if the nation is attacked, then the general leads the soldiers into battle. Naturally, this entails the risk of injury and death, but that is not the purpose of the battle; defeating the enemy is the reason the army was trained, and that is why the officers put the army at risk. Similarly, Jesus became man in order to inaugurate the kingdom of God, but that entailed his entrance into enemy territory: he also needed to defeat Satan and his kingdom of darkness in the world. Therefore, the Holy Spirit led him into direct battle with Satan in order to defeat evil.

Such an understanding does not make the reality of the temptations any easier, any more than understanding the purpose of a war makes the soldier's battle any easier. Jesus would find temptation very difficult as well, as evidenced by the forty days of fasting and hunger. Yet it was out of his own experience that Jesus would later teach us to pray, "Lead us not into temptation" (Matthew 6:13). Just as soldiers are the people most aware of the horrors of war and veterans are the least enthusiastic for it, so Jesus knows the reality of spiritual combat and prays that we be spared of it.

Yet of course we are tempted. Do you ever take the attitude that "God must want me to sin since he let me be tempted"? Do you blame God for the temptations and become angry with him for letting them happen?

What is your experience after giving in to temptation? Does it bring you joy and peace or sorrow and misgivings? Do you take the time to understand your temptation in light of the greater struggle against sin in the world?

Do you see that winning against temptation is worthwhile? Does victory over temptation make you a better, more integrated person? Can you see that overcoming temptation is a victory of God's grace in your life, a victory for his goodness?

Conclude these reflections with an Our Father, focusing on the last two petitions.

_____

_____

_____

_____

Why Was Jesus Tempted by the Devil?

Then Jesus was led up by the Spirit into the wilderness
to be tempted by the devil. (Matthew 4:1)

Consider that Jesus was led into the wilderness to be tempted by the devil. Why the devil? Most of our temptations come from within us—anger, lust, gluttony, selfishness, gossip, and many others. Why did Jesus' temptations not simply come from within himself?

Note that Scripture repeatedly teaches that Jesus is without sin, including original sin. This teaching begins with the prophecy in Isaiah 53:9: "He had done no violence, / and there was no deceit in his mouth." The New Testament states this multiple times, beginning with the good thief who witnessed his death: "This man has done nothing wrong" (Luke 23:41). The same appears many times in various epistles as well:

For our sake he made him to be sin who knew no sin. (2 Corinthians 5:21)

Jesus is a high priest "who in every respect has been tempted as we are, yet without sinning." (Hebrews 4:15)

For it was fitting that we should have such a high priest, holy, blameless, unstained, separated from sinners. (Hebrews 7:26)

He committed no sin; no guile was found on his lips. (1 Peter 2:22, citing Isaiah 53:9)

You know that he appeared to take away sins, and in him there is no sin. (1 John 3:5)

In the face of this biblical truth, we need to reflect more deeply on who Jesus Christ is. A modern tendency has been to treat him as simply just one more human being, though perhaps a bit better than we. In his novel (and the movie based upon it) *The Last Temptation of Christ*, Nikos Kazantzakis portrayed Jesus as having temptations to lust that arise from within himself as he hangs on the cross. This idea is condemned by all Christians, who understand and believe the consistent teaching of Scripture about Jesus being sinless.

Because Jesus is the new Adam (1 Corinthians 15:45), without any sin, he does not have concupiscence, the disordered desires that each of us who are born with original sin experience as temptations from within ourselves. Of course, the interior temptations that come from within ourselves make us more vulnerable to the temptations of the world and the devil. Jesus has no such interior temptation from a fallen, disordered human nature. Rather, his temptations could only come from outside of himself. In the desert, the devil tempted him; later, Peter would tempt him to cease speaking about his upcoming suffering and death, and Jesus would rebuke Peter as "Satan" for doing so (Matthew 16:23). After the multiplication of the loaves, the crowd would tempt him to become a king so that he could give them more bread (John 6:14-15). Yet Jesus does not give in to any of these temptations.

Who do you say Jesus is? St. Peter answered the question this way: "You are the Christ, the Son of the living God" (Matthew 16:16). Yet Jesus often described himself as the "Son of Man." Clearly, Scripture teaches that he is fully God and fully human. And because of his humanity, he understands what we go through. He himself experienced temptation.

Scripture says that Jesus is tempted like us in every way except sin (Hebrew 4:15). How do I understand that? Because he is without sin yet experienced temptations like me, do I turn to him for help? Is Jesus someone to whom I can turn for strength and power in overcoming temptation? Do I know, deep within me, that Jesus understands my own struggles? How often do I turn to him?

Conclude with the prayer the Soul of Christ (see Appendix), slowly considering each aspect of the petitions in regard to your need for strength in overcoming temptation.

_____

_____

_____

_____

_____

_____

_____

_____

_____

_____

_____

_____

_____

Who Is the Devil?

*Then Jesus was led up by the Spirit into the wilderness
to be tempted by the devil. (Matthew 4:1)*

It is the devil who tempts Jesus in this spiritual battle in the wilderness. Who is the devil? While the Hebrew refers to the evil spirit as "Satan," meaning "accuser," the Greek uses the word "*diabolos*," from which comes the English word "devil," meaning, in its secular usage, "prosecuting attorney." This figure is the opposite of the Greek word "*parakletos*," or "paraclete," whose secular meaning is "defense attorney" or "counselor for the defense," and hence "advocate." Jesus is identified in 1 John 2:1 as our "Advocate (*parakletos*) with the Father," and Jesus used the word "*parakletos*" in reference to the Holy Spirit (John 14:16, 26; 15:26; 16:7).

Employing these legal terms, the temptation scene lines up the two sides: Satan is the devil who is the prosecuting attorney, and Jesus Christ is the Advocate who pleads for sinners, "Father, forgive them; for they know not what they do" (Luke 23:34).

Jesus is quite clear in describing his adversary the devil, and we would do well to gain his view of the evil one; this is not some cartoon figure encouraging us merely to be naughty. Rather, we need to learn that he hates each of us and seeks our destruction—and he wants us to become hateful persons ourselves. One of the strongest and clearest teachings about Satan is expressed by Jesus in the Gospel of John:

"You are of your father the devil, and your will is to do your father's desires. He was a murderer from the beginning, and has nothing to do with the truth, because there is no truth in him. When he lies, he speaks according to his own nature, for he is a liar and the father of lies." (8:44)

Jesus' analysis of the devil as "a liar" and the "father of lies" is certainly connected to the "lying spirit" sent to the false prophets who enticed the king of Israel to go into battle, where he would die: "I will go forth, and will be a lying spirit in the mouth of all his [the king's] prophets" (1 Kings 22:22).

Jesus' understanding of the devil as "a murderer from the beginning" (John 8:44) is demonstrated by the devil's influence on Judas Iscariot. Immediately after his discourse on the bread of life, Jesus states, "'Did I not choose you, the twelve, and one of you is a devil?' He spoke of Judas the son of Simon Iscariot, for he, one of the twelve, was to betray him" (John 6:70-71). Interestingly, at the Last Supper when Jesus instituted the Eucharist, John writes, "And during supper, . . . the devil had already put it into the heart of Judas Iscariot, Simon's son, to betray him" (13:2).

Jesus is also very clear that the devil is "the ruler of this world [who shall] be cast out" (John 12:31). Yet he is equally clear that "the ruler of this world . . . has no power over me" (14:30) and that "the ruler of this world is judged" (16:11). Following Jesus' teaching, St. Paul understands the devil as "the god of this world" who "has blinded the minds of the unbelievers, to keep them from seeing the light of the gospel of the glory of Christ, who is the likeness of God" (2 Corinthians 4:4). For that reason, Christian salvation is a deliverance "from the dominion of darkness" to the "kingdom of his beloved Son" (Colossians 1:13). Based on this perspective, Paul teaches Christians what they must do:

Put on the whole armor of God, that you may be able to stand against the wiles of the devil. For we are not contending against flesh and blood, but against the principalities, against the powers, against the world rulers of this present darkness, against the spiritual hosts of wickedness in the heavenly places. (Ephesians 6:11-12)

How seriously do you take the devil and his influence in the world? Do you see him as having as much malicious influence in the world that Jesus and St. Paul say he has?

Are you as aware as Jesus of the devil's deceptive nature? Do you think you are as alert to the deceptive tricks of the devil as Jesus was in his temptations? In your past, have you fallen for demonic lies and falsehoods? What were the ways in which you were tricked? What were the evil one's "empty promises"? What was the result of following his logic into sin?

Do you keep alert to the murderous and death-dealing ways of the devil in the world today? Where do you see these in operation? Have you shared in any of the devil's attitudes or deeds, which may have made you open to hurting others or even yourself? Have you repented for the times that you gave in to the devil's temptation?

Conclude with an Our Father, again focusing on the final two petitions.

_____

_____

_____

_____

The First Temptation

And the tempter came and said to him, "If you are the Son of God, command these stones to become loaves of bread." But he answered, "It is written,

'Man shall not live by bread alone,

but by every word that proceeds from the mouth of God.'"
(Matthew 4:3-4)

Note that the devil is identified as the "tempter," a term also meaning "test." The noun derived from the same root means "temptation" or "trial." The tempter's trick is parallel to the serpent's temptation of Eve: "Did God say, 'You shall not eat of any tree of the garden'?" (Genesis 3:1). Just as the serpent knew the truth of God's word in Eden but posed it as a question, so too here Satan knows Jesus' identity, but he implies doubt: "If you are the Son of God . . . " (Matthew 4:3). Like the prosecuting attorney he is, the devil avoids an outright denial but tries to establish a doubt, and then he demands proof to dispel that doubt by asking Jesus to perform a miracle and turn stones into bread.

From the devil's point of view, this first temptation must have seemed like it would result in an easy victory; after all, Jesus had been fasting for forty days. It parallels the Israelites' craving for bread a month after their departure from Egypt (Exodus 16:1-3) and their later craving for a greater variety of food than the manna, the bread they had been miraculously given (Numbers 11:4-6). Yet notice that the tempter did not ask Jesus to commit a sin but simply to offer proof of his divine Sonship.

Jesus does not engage the temptation or test its inner logic but appeals to a higher principle stated by Moses at the end of the forty years of wandering: "Man shall not live by bread alone, / but by every word that proceeds from the mouth of God" (Matthew 4:4; cf. Deuteronomy 8:3). Part of the relevance of this quotation (and the next two) from Deuteronomy is that Moses spoke these words as a last testament and farewell while the people of Israel dwelt on the plains of Moab. These plains are located across the Jordan River from the Mount of Temptation: Jesus was looking upon the site of Moses' speaking these words as he quoted them.

Another point to remember is that Jesus' answer prepares the Christian believer for a theme that permeates the Gospels—that he has come to accomplish the will of his Father: "I have come down from heaven, not to do my own will, but the will of him who sent me" (John 6:38). Accomplishing the Father's will supersedes his physical need for food, as when Jesus says, "My food is to do the will of him who sent me" (4:24). The devil fails in this temptation to induce Jesus to perform a miracle that satisfies his obvious hunger because Jesus hungers more for his Father's will. He does not need to prove to the devil that he is the Son of God.

Think back on the temptations in your own life. When you examine them closely, do they ever have the quality of being a test intended to trick you?

Consider those temptations that seem to come from physical needs or desires that in themselves are good, such as satisfying hunger. In spite of his obvious hunger, Jesus remained true to his principle of being nourished by doing the Father's will. In what ways have the physical temptations in your life twisted or even perverted the good principles by which you know you should live? Has a legitimate desire for independence through owning property and possessions led you to do something dishonest? Has legitimate desires for love turned into lust that used other people for your own pleasure? Has legitimate self-respect turned into arrogance and a willingness to do anything for other people's approval?

Again, pray the Our Father, with a focus on the first three petitions.

_____

_____

_____

_____

_____

_____

_____

_____

_____

_____

_____

_____

_____

_____

_____

_____

_____

MEDITATION 6

The Second Temptation

Then the devil took him to the holy city, and set him on the pinnacle of the temple, and said to him, "If you are the Son of God, throw yourself down; for it is written,

'He will give his angels charge of you,'
    and
'On their hands they will bear you up,
lest you strike your foot against a stone.'"
Jesus said to him, "Again it is written, 'You shall not tempt
    the Lord your God.'" (Matthew 4:5-7)

The devil continues the same theme of trying to induce Jesus to prove that he is the Son of God. The difference in this second temptation is that the proof will be demonstrated in "the holy city," which is identified as "Jerusalem the holy city" (Isaiah 48:2; 52:1; Nehemiah 11:1; cf. Daniel 9:16), about eighteen miles away from the Mount of Temptation. "The pinnacle of the temple" refers to the high tower on the south wall, traditionally the southeast tower that overlooks the Kidron Valley, lying between the Temple Mount and the Mount of Olives. That high point of the Temple complex standing above the Kidron Valley would have been so prominent that all the people would be able to see such an astonishing miracle of a man surviving a great fall.

The devil entices Jesus with a promise stated in Psalm 91:11-12:

For he will give his angels charge of you / to guard you in all your ways. / On their hands they will bear you up, / lest you dash your foot against a stone.

The devil interprets these verses as particularly applying to the Messiah, whom God's angels will protect from all harm. In fact, this particular temptation is the origin of the popular saying, "Even the devil can quote Scripture."

Once again we can see important connections with the experience of the people of ancient Israel as they departed Egypt. After they reached Mount Sinai and received the commandments and laws of God, the Lord promised to send his angel to protect and guide Israel:

> "Behold, I send an angel before you, to guard you on the way and to bring you to the place which I have prepared. Give heed to him and hearken to his voice, do not rebel against him, for he will not pardon your transgression; for my name is in him.
>
> "But if you hearken attentively to his voice and do all that I say, then I will be an enemy to your enemies and an adversary to your adversaries.
>
> "When my angel goes before you, and brings you in to the Amorites, and the Hittites, and the Perizzites, and the Canaanites, the Hivites, and the Jebusites, and I blot them out, you shall not bow down to their gods, nor serve them, nor do according to their works, but you shall utterly overthrow them and break their pillars in pieces. You shall serve the LORD your God." (Exodus 23:20-25)

However, it is very important to note that the Ten Commandments and the other laws not only preceded the promise of angelic help, but they also established the context and background within which Israel could receive that promise (Exodus 20:1–23:19). Therefore, when the Israelites break the first commandment by making the golden calf, the Lord threatens not to accompany them on their journey to the Promised Land (Exodus 33). The promise is therefore conditional on faithfulness to God and his covenant, as Jesus well understands, but the devil tempts him to forget.

Therefore, Jesus does not seize upon that promise as the devil proposes it. Instead, he again cites Moses' words spoken on the Plains of Moab at the end of Israel's forty-year wandering: "You shall not tempt the Lord your God" (Matthew 4:7; cf. Deuteronomy 6:16). Again, just as God's commandments had preceded the promise of angelic help in Exodus, so too does fidelity to God's will take priority over the promise of angelic help in Psalm 91. One might also note the irony that the devil is tempting the Son of God, thereby breaking the commandment in Deuteronomy 6:16.

Jesus was well aware that the angels were able to help him, as he told Peter in Gethsemane after Peter had cut off the servant's ear:

"Put your sword back into its place; for all who take the sword will perish by the sword. Do you think that I cannot appeal to my Father, and he will at once send me more than twelve legions of angels? But how then should the scriptures be fulfilled, that it must be so?" (Matthew 26:52-54)

However, here too the greater issue was obedience to God's will so as to fulfill it.

Consider times in your life when things were going badly and you wondered, "God, where are you?" Were you tempted to doubt God's existence in a situation of great difficulty, tragedy, or grief? Did you tempt the Lord to prove himself by extricating you from that situation? Did you become angry at God, or even shake a proverbial fist at his silence?

Imagine Jesus kneeling in prayer at the large outcropping of stone known as the "Rock of Agony" in the Garden of Gethsemane, and kneel there with him as he sees an angel strengthening him (Luke 22:43). He knows that legions of angels can protect him from suffering, but one angel offers him a chalice of pain. Speak to him about the times you tempted God by demanding that he help you, and the suffering continued. Let him speak to you about the necessity of fulfilling the Father's will within the wider context of greater goods and the salvation of the world.

Conclude by praying an Our Father with Jesus in Gethsemane.

_____

_____

_____

_____

_____

_____

_____

_____

_____

_____

The Third Temptation

Again, the devil took him to a very high mountain, and showed him all the kingdoms of the world and the glory of them; and he said to him, "All these I will give you, if you will fall down and worship me." Then Jesus said to him, "Begone, Satan! for it is written,

You shall worship the Lord your God
and him only shall you serve.'" (Matthew 4:8-10)

The third temptation is the devil's offer to give Jesus all the kingdoms of the world in exchange for breaking just one commandment, namely, the first commandment that requires Israel to worship the Lord God alone. He presents this small act of worship as a small price to pay compared to "all the kingdoms of the world and the glory of them" (Matthew 4:8).

Note that Jesus does not dispute the devil's claim on all the kingdoms of the world but rather assumes that they are under the devil's authority. The widespread reality of sin certainly confirms demonic influence in the world, and we would do well to reflect on this. Think back on human history. Which culture has been able to avoid violence and the oppression of the weak?

Having analyzed the world well, Jesus clearly taught that the devil is "the ruler of this world [who shall] be cast out" (John 12:31). Similarly, St. Paul, who traveled the Mediterranean world during the famous *Pax Romana,* could still teach that the devil is "the god of this world" who "has blinded the minds of the unbelievers, to keep them from seeing the light of the gospel of the glory of Christ, who is the likeness of God" (2 Corinthians 4:4).

One aspect of the devil's temptation is his assumption that the end justifies the means. Committing a grave sin, such as worshipping him, in order to accomplish God's mission of winning the world for the kingdom of heaven fits perfectly within his mentality. However, if Jesus were to accept the logic of the end justifying the means, he would then belong to the devil's realm of sin and darkness, and by winning the world through a terrible sin, the devil would not lose control of the kingdoms of the world after all. They had become his by tempting people—from the first parents forward—to sin against God in order to gain some apparent good, such as knowing as much as God knows. However, those who fall for his tricks always learn the hard way that they never gain what he has promised, and they lose what they already have.

Jesus refuses the temptation and dismisses Satan, which is the first use of his name in this passage (Matthew 4:10). "Satan" is a Hebrew term meaning "the accuser," and therefore it is just as appropriate as the Greek term "devil." Further, Jesus refutes Satan's temptation by citing Moses a third time: "You shall worship the Lord your God / and him only shall you serve" (Matthew 4:10; cf. Deuteronomy 6:13). The truth of worshipping God alone trumps any offer of an easy way to salvation. Jesus' rejection of this temptation, as well as all other temptations, is the basis of his claim at the Last Supper that "the ruler of this world . . . has no power over me" (John 14:30).

Think back on any temptation you have experienced that were based on the principle of the end justifying the means. If you gave in to the temptation, did it work out for you the way you expected? What has been your experience of giving in to temptation, committing sin, and seeing the way it works out? What lasted longer: the pleasure of the sin or the sense of guilt that followed from the sin?

Consider the times you have heard various promises of "the good life" from people in the world, whether through "friends," the media, or by other means. How did their ideas turn out for you and them?

Think back on the times you did not give in to temptation. What has been the result in your life from those experiences of walking away from some evil that enticed you? Do you still have regrets for not having tried something evil? Do you find more peace from the rejection of a temptation, or more interior agitation? What is the source of either spiritual movement taking place within you?

Conclude with an Our Father.

_____

_____

_____

_____

_____

_____

_____

_____

_____

_____

_____

_____

_____

_____

_____

_____

_____

_____

_____

_____

_____

_____

_____

_____

_____

_____

_____

_____

_____

_____

_____

_____

_____

_____

_____

_____

_____

_____

_____

Aftermath

Then the devil left him, and behold, angels came and ministered to him. (Matthew 4:11)

In the second temptation, the devil suggested that Jesus put his trust in the power of the angels to protect him from falling off the pinnacle of the Temple (Matthew 4:6). Jesus rejected the devil's suggestion to depend on the angels, but now, at the end of the temptations, the angels minister to him to comfort him after the spiritual battle. They show that God's peace follows upon the rejection of temptation, a peace that brings a satisfaction that is always superior to the promise of excitement or other benefits offered by the temptations.

Even more important is that by overcoming the devil's temptations, Jesus has won for us the grace to overcome our temptations. Due to the interior disorder we inherit from original sin (known as concupiscence) and due to past failures to withstand various temptations, both big and small, we tend to be very weak in the face of temptation. However, Jesus' victory over his temptations has become the source of grace upon which we can depend when we are being tempted, whether they are temptations that appeal to bodily needs—such as food, possessions, power, sex, or narcotic substances—or more subtle temptations, such as pride, or spiritual temptations that separate us from the truth of God. Jesus overcame them all, and we spiritual weaklings need to turn to him in our struggle with temptation for the grace to be as victorious as he was.

Another key element demonstrated in these temptations is Jesus' refusal to engage the devil within his own logic of evil and disobedience. We often accept the presuppositions of evil, so we argue within the limitations of its own logic. For example, teenagers are supposedly so driven by "raging hormones" that all that responsible adults can do is provide "protection" and a safe environment for sin; therefore they accept that sexual misbehavior is absolutely inevitable. Such assumptions already grant the higher ground to the enemy of our soul instead of beginning from the inner logic of truth, love, and God himself. In the temptation narratives, we learn from Jesus that an appeal to God's higher logic and deeper truth in scriptural revelation undercuts the devil's assumptions by the finality of God's holy word. Jesus refuted each temptation with quotes from the Book of Deuteronomy (8:3; 6:16; 6:13).

Let us recognize that Jesus' victory over the devil is the beginning of the undoing of the human history of sin and the undoing of our own personal history of sin. Invite Jesus to undo your personal history of failure to overcome temptation, knowing that he can rectify your life by the power of his sinlessness:

> He committed no sin; no guile was found on his lips. When he was reviled, he did not revile in return; when he suffered, he did not threaten; but he trusted to him who judges justly. He himself bore our sins in his body on the tree, that we might die to sin and live to righteousness. By his wounds you have been healed. (1 Peter 2:22-24)

Think about your own temptations, in particular those that you give in to the most frequently or easily. How does the temptation usually begin? What is the sequence of thoughts that takes you step-by-step from acting virtuously to acting sinfully?

Invite Jesus into that scene and observe your sequence of thoughts—that is, the logic of evil—during some recent failures to resist temptation. What might he say to you to unravel those thoughts with the truth from God's word? How might he refute the process of these temptations?

Finally, ask Jesus for his help. Ask that he bestow his grace upon you to have a strength beyond your own ability to reject temptation as he did.

Conclude with the prayer Soul of Christ.

_____

_____

_____

_____

_____

_____

_____

_____

_____

_____

_____

_____

_____

CHAPTER 3

Between Baptism and Capernaum

LUKE 4:14-30

In the Power of the Spirit

And Jesus returned in the power of the Spirit into Galilee, and a report concerning him went out through all the surrounding country. And he taught in their synagogues, being glorified by all. (Luke 4:14-15)

St. Matthew mentions that after Jesus' baptism, his temptations in the wilderness, and the arrest of John the Baptist, he went to Nazareth: "He withdrew into Galilee; and leaving Nazareth he went and dwelt in Capernaum by the sea" (Matthew 4:12-13). While St. Matthew says nothing about this brief time in Nazareth, St. Luke records that Jesus spoke at the synagogue in Nazareth before his move to Capernaum, and St. John relates the story of the wedding in Cana, which is nine miles north of Nazareth. In the next several meditations, we will consider the events that took place in Nazareth.

Luke's summary statement on Jesus' preaching in the synagogues of Galilee highlights his return "in the power of the Spirit" (Luke 4:14). This is the same Holy Spirit by whom his mother conceived him (1:35) and who inspired John the Baptist to leap in his mother's womb and Elizabeth to speak prophetically (1:41-45). The Spirit led Simeon into the Temple to speak with prophetic words (2:25-35), descended on Jesus at his baptism (3:22; Matthew 3:16), and would descend upon the Church on Pentecost (Acts 2:1-4) and direct it throughout its history. In fact, one of the points Jesus will make during his teaching in this synagogue is that the presence and power of the Holy Spirit is a fulfillment of a prophecy and the key to his whole ministry (see the meditation on Luke 4:18-21, page 80).

Jesus shows himself here as a model for every Christian: the leading of the Holy Spirit and his empowerment are necessary for us to live out the calling that the Lord has given us. The Holy Spirit is present and active within us so as to make it possible to live Christian virtues. For that reason, St. Paul describes these virtues as the fruit of the Holy Spirit: "The fruit of the Spirit is love, joy, peace, patience, kindness, goodness, faithfulness, gentleness, self-control" (Galatians 5:22-23). Holiness is primarily not a human accomplishment but a working of the Holy Spirit within our lives. We need the Spirit's help in living out our vocations to marriage and family so that, for instance, even when we do not feel appreciated, we continue to live the virtues necessary and appropriate for that life of generosity. We also need his help to live out the virtues necessary in priestly or religious vocations.

Furthermore, we need the Holy Spirit to empower the ways in which we serve God and others. Many of us are afraid to speak up to promote and defend faith in Jesus Christ in the modern secular culture. Many of us avoid criticizing sinful behavior lest we be accused of being judgmental. Many Christians are afraid of getting involved in helping the poor and disadvantaged because it might become too deep a commitment. Precisely at these points, each of us needs to accept his or her weakness, see it as typical of our fallen human nature, and turn to the Holy Spirit for a strength, knowledge, wisdom, and love that take us beyond what is typical to the level of holiness. Unlike the Blessed Virgin Mary and Jesus, we are not always supple before the Holy Spirit's direction, and we will probably make mistakes. Yet even these become occasions for learning and growing, as was the case for the apostles as related throughout the Gospels and the Acts of the Apostles. Amazingly, they themselves provided the Evangelists with the stories of their failures, their correction by Christ, and their need for repentance. Yet they continued forward to become saints under the direction of the Holy Spirit.

Picture Jesus making his way from the Jordan River to Galilee and back home to Nazareth. He comes "in the power of the Spirit." Would you be able to see the Holy Spirit in Jesus? "A report" (Luke 4:14) about him had circulated throughout the district, and people glorified him as he taught. What would you see in him to indicate that he was empowered by the Holy Spirit?

Now consider your own life. Simply ask God to give you the gift of the Holy Spirit to empower you to live the virtues of holiness and to accomplish the tasks of your mission from God. If you have already received the Sacrament of Confirmation, ask the Lord to stir up the gift of the Holy Spirit you received in that sacrament. (If you have not received Confirmation, go seek it out!)

When you ask for the power of the Holy Spirit, what do you think you will see in your life? He will remain as invisible to you as he was in Jesus, yet what effects do you expect to come about within you? Recall the fruits of the Spirit (Galatians 5:22-23) —"love, joy, peace, patience, kindness, goodness, faithfulness, gentleness, self-control" —and ask yourself, "In which of these do I need to grow the most?"

Conclude with the prayer Come, Holy Spirit or the hymn "Come Holy Ghost."

_____

_____

_____

MEDITATION 2

In the Synagogue in Nazareth

And he came to Nazareth, where he had been brought up; and he went to the synagogue, as his custom was, on the sabbath day. And he stood up to read; and there was given to him the book of the prophet Isaiah. He opened the book and found the place where it was written . . . (Luke 4:16-17)

Luke states, after the presentation in the Temple (2:22-40) and the finding of Jesus in the Temple (2:41-52) and here as well, that Nazareth is the place of Jesus' upbringing. Perhaps three or four hundred people lived in this village at the time of Christ. Many homes, as archaeologists have uncovered, were attached to caves, which are cooler in summer and warmer in winter. The name "Nazareth" is connected to the Hebrew root "*netzer*," meaning a "shoot" of a tree or branch, and may be connected to Isaiah 11:1, which prophesies that the Messiah would be a "shoot from the stump of Jesse." Perhaps the name "Nazareth" expressed the people's hope for the coming of the Messiah.

Attendance at the synagogue, which was a Pharisaic institution, was Jesus' custom, and his return home did not change that. This episode and others indicate that Jesus and the early Church attended synagogues as part of their intimate connection with Israel. Yet as Luke 4:15 states, the synagogue was more than the site of customary worship: this was where Jesus exercised his mission to preach repentance and the coming of the kingdom of God.

Jesus was given the scroll of the prophet Isaiah to read, perhaps as part of the Pharisees' lectionary. The Torah (the first five books of the Bible) remain the core source for Jewish teaching; the Pharisees organized the Torah into a lectionary that presented all five books in a regular cycle of readings. Readings from the prophets and the psalms, known as "*haphtoroth*," supplemented the Torah texts each week. No clear evidence for a *haphtorah* cycle exists for this period, so perhaps Jesus could choose the passage he wanted from the Isaiah scroll that had been handed to him. At the very least, this passage shows that Jesus knew how to read, just as John 8:6-9 shows that he could write.

We can reflect on Jesus' custom of weekly attendance at the synagogue and his regular practice of going to the synagogues to read the Scriptures and preach to people. Many Christians place themselves above such a custom of weekly Mass attendance, often claiming that they do not get anything out of it. Sometimes it seems that the same things are said every week, and the Scriptures do not capture their imagination. However, St. Luke informs us here that Jesus was not above such a habit. Even though he ran into a variety of controversies at the various synagogues he attended (including this one at Nazareth), he continued his custom.

Look at your own experience of attending weekly Mass. How alert are you to the Scripture texts that are proclaimed each week? How often do you prepare yourself to hear them by reading and praying over them before you come to church? Do you continue to reflect on them during the week after the Sunday celebration? Do you look for ways to apply the Scriptures to your own life?

Jesus also saw the synagogue as the place of his mission to the people of Israel. Have you ever considered your fellow parishioners as the area of the mission God has given you? Have you ever considered becoming a lector at Mass? Have you considered teaching catechism to the children or leading an adult Bible study in your parish? Have you considered volunteering to visit the shut-ins of the parish or taking responsibility for giving an elderly or disabled person a ride to Mass each week? What might you learn if you took up such a mission? How might you grow?

Imagine Jesus sitting with you in your parish church, and ask him what he might want you to do at this stage of your life, speaking to him as a friend to a Friend.

Conclude with the prayer Soul of Christ.

_____

_____

_____

_____

_____

_____

_____

_____

_____

_____

_____

_____

_____

_____

Jesus Reads Isaiah

"The Spirit of the Lord is upon me,
because he has anointed me to preach good news to the poor.
He has sent me to proclaim release to the captives
and recovering of sight to the blind,
to set at liberty those who are oppressed,
to proclaim the acceptable year of the Lord."
And [Jesus] closed the book, and gave it back to the attendant, and
sat down; and the eyes of all in the synagogue were fixed on him.
And he began to say to them, "Today this scripture has been fulfilled in your hearing." (Luke 4:18-21)

Jesus looked for and found the above passage from the
prophet Isaiah (61:1-2, and a partial line from 58:6), which
he read to the congregation, composed of the people of Nazareth with whom he had prayed ever since his arrival there.
Within that context, he reads the text to explain that he has
changed. Before his baptism by John in the Jordan, he was the
local carpenter ("Joseph's son"—Luke 4:22); now he is a highly
honored teacher in synagogues throughout Galilee.

The key to understanding this transformation is the line "The
Spirit of the Lord is upon me" (Luke 4:18). The people of Nazareth had not witnessed the descent of the Holy Spirit upon Jesus
as he left the waters of the Jordan, so this is news to them. Yet
it is precisely the gift of the Spirit that fulfills this prophecy, and
before the congregation Jesus makes it clear that "today this
scripture has been fulfilled" in him (4:21).

Isaiah's prophetic words also announce a program of action that makes better sense in light of the phrase "the acceptable year of the Lord." This is a reference to Israel's commandment to celebrate the Jubilee every fifty years (Leviticus 25:10-55). Why does Jesus include a reference about the Jubilee? The passage in Isaiah, which could be referring to the Jubilee of 473 BC, the first Jubilee after the returned Jewish exiles had rebuilt the Temple in 516 BC, is chosen by Jesus to indicate that his ministry is the start of the greatest Jubilee of all—his public ministry, death, and resurrection.

This provides some context for understanding the promise of "good news to the poor," "release to the captives," "recovering of sight," and setting "at liberty" the oppressed within the "acceptable year of the Lord" (Luke 4:18-19). Every fifty years the Jubilee set things right and provided a new beginning for the poor and the enslaved. At that time, people could become, in effect, indentured servants, selling themselves into slavery for seven years if they went bankrupt. And while impoverished people could "sell" their land, this sale was considered more like a lease, since the Lord had distributed the land as a permanent heritage for each tribe and clan. In the Jubilee Year, slaves were freed and land that had been bought was restored to the previous owners. Jesus, by his death and resurrection, would give sinners a new start as well—by offering them a true forgiveness that the Temple sacrifices were incapable of bestowing.

"Sight to the blind" is not mentioned in the Hebrew text of Isaiah 61:1-2, but the idea is repeated in Isaiah 35:5 and 42:16-18, which are prophecies of messianic times. Opening the eyes of the blind and healing those who were lame, paralyzed, deaf, or sick would all be part of Jesus' Jubilee mission, as empowered and directed by the Holy Spirit, who had anointed him at the word of the Father. In this way, we can also see Jesus' ministry as a Trinitarian ministry.

Jesus sat down with all eyes upon him as he announced that this Scripture was being fulfilled "today." How were his fellow citizens to react?

Imagine yourself sitting in the synagogue—a small rectangular building in the village. Listen to Jesus reading the Isaiah text and announcing that he has fulfilled it. Remain focused on Jesus as he says those words, and consider your own reaction. What do you think about his claim of fulfilling ancient prophecies from the Old Testament? Enter more deeply into considering the impact this has on your faith in Jesus.

Then speak to Jesus about what the fulfillment of this prophecy means to you. Consider each aspect of the Jubilee promises about which Isaiah wrote. What do these promises mean for your understanding of Jesus' ministry? What does his announcement of the Spirit being upon him mean to you? How is he freeing you? Healing you? Speak to him about these things. What does he say to you?

Conclude with the prayer Soul of Christ.

_____

_____

_____

_____

_____

_____

A Superficial Familiarity with Jesus

And all spoke well of him, and wondered at the gracious words which proceeded out of his mouth; and they said, "Is not this Joseph's son?" And he said to them, "Doubtless you will quote to me this proverb, 'Physician, heal yourself; what we have heard you did at Capernaum, do here also in your own country.'" And he said, "Truly, I say to you, no prophet is acceptable in his own country." (Luke 4:22-24)

The first reaction of the synagogue listeners is approval, with a sense of wonder at these "gracious words" that came from Jesus. Their rhetorical question—"Is not this Joseph's son?" (Luke 4:22)—is more a statement that he is someone with whom they are quite familiar. Yet he speaks in a way that is most unfamiliar.

Though no one has explicitly stated the proverb "Physician, heal yourself" (Luke 4:23), Jesus is certain that the congregation will expect the same kinds of miracles in Nazareth that they have heard about from his ministry elsewhere in Galilee, especially in Capernaum. While the people demand healings and miracles, Jesus demands faith from them first. Rather typical of Middle Eastern argumentation, he responds with another proverb: "No prophet is acceptable in his own country" (4:24).

This saying applies not only to Jesus' fellow citizens in Nazareth but also to those today who have grown up in a Christian culture. Most modern people have a certain familiarity with Jesus. They see his image in churches, in art, and in the Christmas crèche. But such pseudofamiliarity with Jesus without listening to him can give us an understanding of Jesus that is as superficial as that of the people of Nazareth. We might think we know all about him already and yet fail to pray, profess our faith in him, or repent of our sins to him. We might blame him when things go badly in life and yet forget to thank him for the good he does in our lives.

Think about the ways in which many modern people are just like the people of Nazareth—they think they know Jesus; they think they have him pegged. They might admit that he is the Christ, but they avoid expressing a saving, trusting faith in him. How does Jesus' proverb about being an unwelcome prophet apply to such people? Try to imagine specific people you know or encounter who act in such a way. How would you try to share your own faith and knowledge of Jesus with them? What would you say about Jesus to them?

Then consider your own attitudes toward Jesus. In what ways has any form of superficial familiarity with Jesus become a block to your own faith commitment to him? Think of times when you approve of him on one level, and you want him to do various signs and miracles to help you, but you do not let him be the center of your life or the One whose guidance is most important of all in your life.

Ask Jesus for the grace of deeper faith. Rather than remaining at the level of unbelief as in Nazareth (Matthew 13:58; Mark 6:6), pray, "I believe, but help my unbelief" (Mark 9:24).

Conclude with the prayer Soul of Christ.

_____

_____

_____

The People React

"But in truth, I tell you, there were many widows in Israel in the days of Elijah, when the heaven was shut up three years and six months, when there came a great famine over all the land; and Elijah was sent to none of them but only to Zarephath, in the land of Sidon, to a woman who was a widow. And there were many lepers in Israel in the time of the prophet Elisha; and none of them was cleansed, but only Naaman the Syrian." When they heard this, all in the synagogue were filled with wrath. And they rose up and put him out of the city, and led him to the brow of the hill on which their city was built, that they might throw him down headlong. But passing through the midst of them he went away. (Luke 4:25-30)

Jesus illustrates his proverb about the prophet who is unwelcome in his own country with examples from the lives of Elijah and Elisha. The people of Israel had rejected both prophets, but they became instruments of God's miracles for foreigners—the Canaanite widow of Zarephath and the Syrian general Naaman who had leprosy.

These examples clearly compare the congregation in Nazareth to the ancient Israelites who had worshipped Baal rather than accepting Elijah and Elisha as true prophets of the Lord God. After listening to Jesus, the people of Nazareth became so angry that they "rose up" to kill him (Luke 4:29). However, with the superior strength of the Holy Spirit with whom he had been anointed, Jesus walks through the midst of the angry crowd. He does not fight and he does not run; with a hidden power he simply walks away.

Consider how this episode looks backward and forward in Luke's Gospel. From the backward perspective, we call to mind Simeon's prediction in the Temple to Christ's mother: "This child is set for the fall and rising of many in Israel" (Luke 2:34). In this first example of Christ's preaching, the people in Nazareth reject Jesus, thereby ensuring their "fall."

This text also looks forward to the rest of Jesus' ministry in the Gospel. Think about the various ways in which some hearers fall to anger and reject Jesus while others rise to faith in him. This continues right through his crucifixion, when one of the condemned thieves crucified with Jesus ridicules his power to help while the other asks to be with him in paradise.

Begin by considering the ways in which contemporary society wants to throw Jesus off the cliff. Where does our culture institutionalize rejection of faith in God? In what ways might Jesus be calling you to change the culture? Speak to Jesus about the rejection you might feel because of your faith. Recall one instance when you have felt belittled, ignored, or ridiculed. What does Jesus say to you? How does he want you to respond the next time that happens?

Look at your life through the lens of the ways in which you have accepted or rejected Jesus. When you accept Jesus, how does he make you "rise" in life? When you reject Jesus, in what ways do you experience a "fall"? What does he say to you? How do you respond to him?

Conclude with the prayer Soul of Christ.

CHAPTER 4

The Wedding Feast at Cana

JOHN 2:1-11

Jesus the Bridegroom

On the third day there was a marriage at Cana in Galilee, and
the mother of Jesus was there; Jesus also was invited to the marriage, with his disciples. (John 2:1-2)

Cana is not far from Nazareth, just a few hours' walk. St.
John immediately moves to establish the main characters
of this episode: the mother of Jesus, who throughout his
Gospel remains unnamed, Jesus, and his disciples. Identifying
these persons, with no concern for the identity or relationship
of the couple being married, their families, or the other guests,
is a way to highlight the importance of the truly main characters. At most wedding celebrations, the bride and groom, or at
least their parents who make the feast possible, are the center of
attention. Here that is not so.

Jesus accepted the invitation to the wedding, thereby showing his willingness to share in the life of a new family and its
promise of new life. While rabbis and priests were especially
expected to marry and have children, Jesus remained unmar-
ried, a very unusual state for most Jews except the Essenes,
whose core community was celibate. Still, he always taught
that the married state was a good to be protected. In the Ser-
mon on the Mount, he spoke strongly against divorce, even
when the law permitted it (Matthew 5:31-32; contrast with
Deuteronomy 24:1-4), and he supported marriage as a lifelong
covenant based on God's purpose at the creation (Matthew
19:7-9). Here his presence at a wedding is a sign of his cher-
ishing the union of man and woman as well as family, and his

presence is considered a blessing, not just to one couple, but to all marriages.

Yet it would not be entirely correct to see Jesus as a single man. He identified himself as a "bridegroom" whose presence causes his disciples to rejoice instead of fasting (Matthew 9:15). He describes heaven as the wedding feast of a king's son (22:2), clearly referring to himself. John the Baptist identifies Jesus as the Bridegroom while John is merely the Bridegroom's friend (John 3:29).

This Gospel teaching about Jesus as the Bridegroom then leads us to ask, "Who is the bride of Jesus Christ?" Based on the teachings of the prophets that Israel is the bride of the Lord God (Hosea 1-3; Jeremiah 2:2; Ezekiel 16; Isaiah 54; 62:3-5), St. Paul and St. John speak of Christ as the Bridegroom and the Church as his bride:

> I feel a divine jealousy for you, for I betrothed you to Christ to present you as a pure bride to her one husband. (2 Corinthians 11:2)

> "For this reason a man shall leave his father and mother and be joined to his wife, and the two shall become one flesh." This is a great mystery, and I mean in reference to Christ and the church. (Ephesians 5:31-32)

> Let us rejoice and exult and give him the glory, / for the marriage of the Lamb has come, / and his Bride has made herself ready; / it was granted her to be clothed with fine linen, bright and pure"— / for the fine linen is the righteous deeds of the saints. / And the angel said to me, "Write this: Blessed are those who are invited

to the marriage supper of the Lamb." And he said to me, "These are true words of God." (Revelation 19:7-9)

And I saw the holy city, new Jerusalem, coming down out of heaven from God, prepared as a bride adorned for her husband; and I heard a great voice from the throne saying, "Behold, the dwelling of God is with men. He will dwell with them, and they shall be his people, and God himself will be with them; he will wipe away every tear from their eyes, and death shall be no more, neither shall there be mourning nor crying nor pain any more, for the former things have passed away." (Revelation 21:2-4)

In light of these images of marriage, consider that Jesus' presence (and the miracle he is about to perform) at the wedding feast of Cana blesses not only that couple but all marriages. Consider further that Jesus teaches, and his disciples later develop, the truth that he is not a bachelor but a Bridegroom who postpones marriage for the kingdom of heaven. Jesus will be espoused for all eternity to his bride, the Church, in the ultimate feast at the consummation of the world and all history.

Place yourself with Jesus in his role as the Bridegroom. What kind of relationship does he have with the Church that he considers his bride? Speak to him about your own relationship to the Church: do you think of it more in terms of an organization and bureaucracy, or do you look at the Church through Jesus' Bridegroom eyes? Sometimes the guests at a wedding may engage in their own evaluation of a bride, but how does the groom see her? Now ask yourself: are you like a guest who evaluates Christ's bride and judges her from a distance? Or do you see yourself as a member of the Church, who is Christ's bride? Imagine the Bridegroom's gaze into the eyes of his Church. Do you experience yourself as a member of the Church who reciprocates that gaze of love?

Conclude with the prayer Soul of Christ, prayed as a member of Christ's bride.

Another approach to this scene is to consider Jesus' attitude toward marriage. What does his teaching about his spousal relationship to the Church convey to you about marriage? The portrayal of the end of the world as a wedding feast indicates that marriage is one of the signs of the ultimate consummation of love between God and the Church.

Speak to Jesus about the way he cherishes marriage as a vocation to which he calls people. Why is this vocation a gift, and what fruit does he seek from it? What does he desire for couples who are called to marriage? What is his vision for their children? What mission does he present to married couples and families in their service to the larger society? What does he ask of you in regard to your own attitude towards matrimony as a sacrament and a vocation?

Conclude with Psalm 45, which was composed for the king's wedding.

_____

_____

_____

_____

_____

Jesus' Mother Presents Him with a Problem

When the wine failed, the mother of Jesus said to him,
"They have no wine." (John 2:3)

The mother of Jesus, who is otherwise simply one more guest among many, gets the first point of attention in the scene at the wedding at Cana. This is because the wine is no longer flowing, and she is acutely attentive to the needs of other people, in this case, the hosts. She does not consult with the hosts, who would normally be expected to do something about this embarrassing problem, but instead, she consults with Jesus, simply stating the problem: "They have no wine" (John 2:3). It is important to note that her first words in the Gospel are a statement of the crisis; she does not suggest any program for solving it, nor does she tell Jesus what to do. So many people pray for help from God, and their prayers frequently try to direct God on how to solve the problem. Mother Mary does not do that at all, but leaves her Son's response completely open to his decision.

Place yourself in the scene where Jesus' mother approaches him. What is her expression? Pay attention to her alertness to the needs of others and to her readiness to bring those needs to Jesus. Ask yourself whether you are as ready to bring the needs of others to Jesus when you are alerted to them. What motivates you, either to bring him your needs or not? Do you try not to "bother" Jesus if you judge the need too small? If you bring your needs to Jesus, do you come also with a description of the solution as you understand it? Do you find that the Lord answers prayers in the way you tell him to do so?

Consider past occasions when the Lord did answer your petitions. What strikes you about the way in which he chose to bring about the answer? What about the timing of the answer—how did that work out? Speak to Jesus about the ways in which he has already answered your prayers. What might he say to you about your way of offering petitions? What kind of trust does he want to evoke from you?

Conclude with a Hail Mary and an Our Father.

_____

_____

_____

_____

_____

_____

_____

_____

_____

_____

_____

_____

_____

_____

_____

_____

_____

_____

_____

_____

_____

Jesus Responds to His Mother

And Jesus said to her, "O woman, what have you to do with me? My hour has not yet come." His mother said to the servants, "Do whatever he tells you." (John 2:4-5)

The literal translation of Jesus' response to his mother uses a standard idiom that is found elsewhere in the Bible: "What to me and to you?" Sometimes it is said by a person who has been harmed by another, making it a hostile phrase (Judges 11:12; 1 Kings 17:18; 2 Chronicles 35:21; demons speaking to Jesus in Mark 1:24; 5:7) Other times it indicates disengagement from someone because the matter at hand does not concern the person (2 Kings 3:13; Hosea 14:8). Or it can mean that the matter at hand is of no importance to either party (2 Samuel 16:10). This last meaning best fits Jesus' response to his mother-in-law in John 2:4.

Jesus then gives his mother the reason for his disengagement: "My hour has not yet come" (John 2:4). Jesus says the same thing elsewhere, as in John 7:6, and St. John repeats the idea in his editorial comments:

So they sought to arrest him; but no one laid hands on him, because his hour had not yet come. (John 7:30)

These words he spoke in the treasury, as he taught in the temple; but no one arrested him, because his hour had not yet come. (John 8:20)

When Jesus does say his hour has come, it refers to the time of his death.

> "The hour has come for the Son of man to be glorified. Truly, truly, I say to you, unless a grain of wheat falls into the earth and dies, it remains alone; but if it dies, it bears much fruit. He who loves his life loses it, and he who hates his life in this world will keep it for eternal life. If any one serves me, he must follow me; and where I am, there shall my servant be also; if any one serves me, the Father will honor him.
>
> "Now is my soul troubled. And what shall I say? 'Father, save me from this hour'? No, for this purpose I have come to this hour. Father, glorify thy name." Then a voice came from heaven, "I have glorified it, and I will glorify it again." (John 12:23-28)

At the beginning of the Last Supper discourse, St. John states this:

> Now before the feast of the Passover, when Jesus knew that his hour had come to depart out of this world to the Father, having loved his own who were in the world, he loved them to the end. (John 13:1)

Within the context of John's Gospel, the "hour" clearly refers to Christ's death. Therefore, Jesus is informing his mother that her statement about the lack of wine implies a request that Jesus perceives as the initiation of his hour, the hour of his death. This becomes all the more poignant in that the only other mention of his mother occurs when she is standing at the cross during "that hour" (John 19:26-27).

Jesus' mother does not tell him what to do; she tells the servants to obey Jesus. She obviously trusts that he will do his heavenly Father's will regarding his "hour," in an appropriate response to the family's embarrassing situation. By saying to the servants, "Do whatever he tells you" (John 2:5), she provides a model for every believer to trust in Jesus' wisdom and understanding of the Father's will. Later, as Jesus begins the journey to Jerusalem and his death, his Father will give the same message at the Transfiguration—"This is my beloved Son; listen to him" (Mark 9:7). Each person needs to heed the words of Mary and the Father and listen to and obey Jesus.

Again, imagine yourself standing nearby and overhearing this part of the conversation between Jesus and his mother. Consider the way both of them seek to do the Father's will. Jesus' hour, which has been appointed by the Father as the hour of his dying in order to redeem the world, has not yet come. Performing a miracle will initiate the hour in some way, known only to Jesus at this point. His mother still does not lay out what action she wants him to take but simply tells the servants to do whatever he asks. She is not insisting on her will but is trusting Jesus to do the Father's will.

What level of openness to God's will do you experience in your prayers of petition or in your seeking out the will of God for your life? Do you share the attitude of Jesus and his mother in regard to doing the Father's will, or do you insist on telling God to do your will?

Imagine yourself speaking to the Blessed Virgin Mary about Jesus' words to her: "What to me and to you? My hour has not yet come." What may have gone on in her mind? What might she say to you about your attitude toward Jesus' responses to your petitions? Say a Hail Mary.

Then imagine yourself speaking to Jesus about his hour when he answers your needs. What might he say to you about your attitude toward the Father's will as the context of your petitions and needs?

Conclude with an Our Father, focusing on the first three petitions.

_____

_____

_____

_____

_____

_____

_____

_____

_____

_____

_____

_____

_____

_____

_____

_____

_____

MEDITATION 4

Jesus Acts to Resolve the Problem

Now six stone jars were standing there, for the Jewish rites of purification, each holding twenty or thirty gallons. Jesus said to them, "Fill the jars with water." And they filled them up to the brim. He said to them, "Now draw some out, and take it to the steward of the feast." So they took it. When the steward of the feast tasted the water now become wine, and did not know where it came from (though the servants who had drawn the water knew), the steward of the feast called the bridegroom and said to him, "Every man serves the good wine first; and when men have drunk freely, then the poor wine; but you have kept the good wine until now." This, the first of his signs, Jesus did at Cana in Galilee, and manifested his glory; and his disciples believed in him. (John 2:6-11)

St. John mentions six stone water jars for the "Jewish rites of purification" (John 2:6). The Mishna, a set of rabbinic teachings, mentions that unclean water may be rendered clean "by contact in a stone vessel." Furthermore, Jewish custom includes important points about ritual washing of hands and serving vessels, so the ritually clean water in stone jars would have been necessary at a large gathering. Here, Jesus orders the servants to fill the six large jars to the brim, thereby rendering the water ritually clean, in accord with the tradition.

The description of this miracle is very restrained: no mention is made of a change in color or any other quality. Jesus simply orders the servants to "draw some out" and give it to the steward (John 2:8). Following the command of Jesus' mother, the servants do what Jesus tells them.

At this point, the chief steward tastes the water turned into wine and is so moved by its superior quality that he addresses the bridegroom, whom he believes has foolishly offered the poorer quality wine before the better, contrary to good sense. However, neither man knows anything about the transformation; only Jesus and the servants who obeyed his mother and him are aware of the miraculous nature of the event.

In yet another aspect of Jesus' blessing of this marriage, both the superb quality and the extravagant amount of wine are his gift. This, too, is a sign of his blessing on all marriages.

The episode concludes by stating that Jesus "manifested his glory; and his disciples believed in him" (John 2:11). The miracle evoked an act of faith, because the disciples did not merely enjoy the best wine they had ever tasted but recognized this as a sign of Christ's identity. Yet this is a beginning act of faith and by no means the last time the disciples will profess faith in Jesus. The frequent mention of their acts of faith throughout the Gospels indicates to us that faith can continue to grow and mature, perhaps like a good wine.

Consider the interplay of characters in this last part of the scene. The servants simply obey Jesus, probably with little comprehension of the purpose of his orders. Yet as servants they are obedient and play their part. Have you ever been in the position of such servants, simply doing what you are told and playing a role you did not understand until after you had finished doing your duties? When you look at such occasions, how did you feel? Did you thank God for the grace of obedience and for the privilege of taking part in accomplishing his will?

Consider the chief steward and the bridegroom. Neither is aware of the miracle that has taken place. The steward simply speaks of the wisdom he possesses based on past experience, but his lack of awareness of Jesus' miracle makes him sound as ignorant and foolish as he accuses the bridegroom of being. Have you been in similar circumstances in which you made assumptions about a situation while not knowing what God had already done? How did you come to realize that your lack of faith and knowledge of God's activity had limited your perspective on a situation? How did that realization open you to deeper faith?

Finally, think of yourself in the disciples' position: though they were in the background as Jesus and his mother spoke and as the servants, steward, and groom interacted, they observed what had happened and responded with faith in Jesus—they "believed in him" (John 2:11). Yet earlier, the very fact that they had already begun to follow him meant that they had faith. At Cana it grew; it would grow to new levels throughout their lives, sometimes punctuated with moments of doubt.

Think back on when your faith began. What was the earliest act of faith you can remember? Picture that scene again, with Jesus standing there (as he surely was doing). What first attracted you to him? Recall the subsequent experiences of coming to new levels of faith, and speak to Jesus within each of these moments, knowing that he is present. Converse with him about the moments that sustain your faith and the moments that challenge it.

The peace and satisfaction of faith in childhood get challenged when we become adolescents and young adults, especially when we go from merely having questions about life to questioning life itself. As one works through those questions, a new level of faith becomes necessary. Later stages of adulthood bring new questions as well. As we raise families, our faith includes a sense of providence for the care of each family member, especially for our children. In middle age, we usually evaluate how our adulthood has succeeded or failed, and we begin to look at the meaning and importance of the second half of life. Later, we deal with illness, infirmity, and the increasingly frequent experience of the loss of loved ones as the inevitability of our own death approaches. At each stage, we grow in faith, and we need to grow, not rejecting all that has gone before, but integrating it all.

Ask for grace to continue the process of growth, and conclude with a Hail Mary and an Our Father.

_____

_____

_____

_____

_____

_____

_____

_____

_____

_____

_____

_____

_____

CHAPTER 5

Jesus Inaugurates His Public Ministry

MATTHEW 4:12-25

Darkness and the Shadow of Death

Now when he heard that John had been arrested, he withdrew into Galilee; and leaving Nazareth he went and dwelt in Capernaum by the sea, in the territory of Zebulun and Naphtali, that what was spoken by the prophet Isaiah might be fulfilled:
"The land of Zebulun and the land of Naphtali,
toward the sea, across the Jordan,
Galilee of the Gentiles—
the people who sat in darkness
have seen a great light,
and for those who sat in the region and shadow of death
light has dawned." (Matthew 4:12-16)

The arrest of John the Baptist by Herod Antipas in Judea signals a new stage for Jesus' ministry up north in Galilee where his mission will begin. The ministry of the Forerunner, John, is over, and the ministry of the Messiah now begins. John's arrest is recounted in the Gospels (Matthew 11:2; 14:3-4; Mark 1:14; 6:17; Luke 3:20) and was known to the Jewish historian Josephus, who wrote that Herod imprisoned John in the desert fortress of Machaerus (Muqawir in modern Jordan), far from the people and any attempts to free him. In this context, Jesus' move to Galilee is not flight away from Herod Antipas but rather an embrace of his mission, as prophesied in Isaiah 9:1-2 and cited in Matthew 4:15-16.

Isaiah spoke this prophecy during the Assyrian invasion of northern Israel in 734–732 BC, during which two-thirds of the kingdom was taken from Israel. This was the original reason that Isaiah identified Galilee as belonging to the Gentiles. Later in history, the Iturean Gentiles entered Galilee to farm its very rich land. However, in 104 BC, Judah Aristobulus, then the king and high priest of Judea, conquered the Itureans in Galilee. He forced them to be circumcised and practice Judaism. This forced conversion helps to explain why the Galilean Jews were considered inferior by the Judeans and is part of the background for the application of this prophecy from Isaiah 9:1-2 to Jesus' ministry.

The Gentile background of many Jews living in Galilee, plus the presence of the Roman oppressors in the region, especially in Sepphoris (very close to Nazareth), Tiberias (on the Sea of Galilee), and even in Capernaum, accounts for the description of Galilee as a place where people "sat in darkness" and as a "region" in the "shadow of death" (Matthew 4:16). Yet Jesus chooses to go to this very region to be the light that will shine on these people. He will walk from Nazareth to Capernaum, a journey through the broad and fertile valley of the tribal region of Zebulun and, as the land goes down toward the Sea of Galilee, into the territory of Naphtali, to fulfill Isaiah's prophecy through his ministry. (Though both tribes were among the ten lost tribes of Israel who had been taken captive by the Assyrians and never returned, the names of their tribal territories remained.)

We would do well to consider the ways in which Isaiah's prophecy about the darkness in Galilee persisted through different historical epochs, whether applying it to the Assyrian invasion, the Iturean intrusion, or the Roman occupation. Similarly, identifying a region or time period as belonging to "darkness" and "the shadow of death" can apply to all regions and periods of time throughout the world. Many modern people have trouble accepting the application of "darkness" and "shadow of death" to their own age because they hold the myth that the progress of science and technology is wiping out ignorance, superstition, and barbarity. However, a closer look at modern history shows that the shadow of death has stretched well into each New Year celebration. Wars, terrorism, the drug trade, corruption in government and some large businesses, the disregard for the needs of the poor and care of the environment, the widespread acceptance of licentious behavior and abortion—the shadow of death still lengthens.

Imagine the darkness and deadly shadows of today's world. Which areas of darkness seem prominent or most worrisome to you at the present? Now imagine Jesus our Lord walking like a great light into those dark areas of our society. Perhaps see him walking to the abortion clinics, past the porn filmmakers, the drug dealers, the murderers, the corrupt politicians and business people, the terrorists, or any other shadowy place. See Jesus walk through these as he walked through Galilee. Speak to him about the situations you picture. What would he say to you about each dark shadow of the world? What does he want to say to this world?

Conclude with an Our Father, saying it along with Jesus.

_____

_____

_____

_____

_____

_____

_____

The Call to Repent

From that time Jesus began to preach, saying, "Repent, for the kingdom of heaven is at hand." (Matthew 4:17)

This Scripture verse summarizes Jesus' message: "Repent, for the kingdom of heaven is at hand." This is the radiance of his light shining among the people of Galilee. The word "repent" is a plural imperative, giving an order rather than a plea to everyone who hears him. "Repent" is a word meaning "turn around," based on the image of people who are following a wrong path. It is not sufficient for them to recognize that their path is incorrect; that is a first step in repentance. Everyone following a path of sin needs to recognize that it can only lead to bad results, usually with increasing pain along the way, and eventually to destruction.

Often people reach that insight by observing the catastrophes that sin brings to the lives of other people. Sometimes people feel the pain caused by their own sins—the misery of a hangover, the loss of property from excessive gambling, the folly of the materialistic acquisition of useless possessions, loneliness after broken relationships, the diseases resulting from sexual misconduct, or any of the many other destructive results of sin. At those points, people can repent, that is, turn around from that path of destructive sin by backtracking to the path that leads to eternal life within the kingdom of God that Jesus brings near to them.

As folks have done repeatedly in past centuries, we can avoid Jesus' command to repent in two ways. The more important avoidance takes the shape of denying our own need to repent.

We can put up a variety of defenses against recognizing our moral guilt and culpability for sin. We can refuse to look honestly at our own behavior or rationalize it in any number of ways. We can blame someone else for what we have done.

The second avoidance of Jesus' command to repent occurs when we seek to redefine "sin." Some teach that the modern world has so changed that sins of the past are no longer sinful. Instead of calling the world to repent, they accept the world's ideas, especially with the issues of sexuality, human reproduction, and life. However, the terrible consequences of our behaviors will happen whether or not we consider them sins. And those groups that have most accommodated the culture are often losing large chunks of their membership; they have not won the world to themselves.

First and most important, imagine Jesus walking into the areas of darkness in your own life and telling you, "Repent, for the kingdom of heaven is at hand." From what kinds of shadows is Jesus calling you to "turn around" in order to repent? What is the path that has led you into dark shadows of sin? Think back on what the promise of the sin has been, and then consider how it turned out. Let Jesus help you notice the wrong turns you have made in your life, and speak to him about what exactly was wrong with them.

Then picture him leading you as you retrace your steps away from that wrong, sinful path. As the paths of sin are left behind, take notice of the new path that Jesus offers—a narrow road that looks difficult at first but that leads to heaven (Matthew 7:13-14). With that choice in front of you, do you want to follow Jesus and walk the narrow path to heaven in his light? Is heaven worthwhile enough for you to make that journey with Jesus? Or do you want to return to the dark path of sin that leads to death? What do you say to Jesus about this choice? What does he say to you?

Conclude by praying Psalm 23.

_____

_____

_____

_____

_____

_____

_____

_____

_____

_____

_____

_____

_____

_____

_____

_____

_____

_____

_____

_____

Jesus Calls the First Four Disciples

As he walked by the Sea of Galilee, he saw two brothers, Simon who is called Peter and Andrew his brother, casting a net into the sea; for they were fishermen. And he said to them, "Follow me, and I will make you fishers of men." Immediately they left their nets and followed him. And going on from there he saw two other brothers, James the son of Zebedee and John his brother, in the boat with Zebedee their father, mending their nets, and he called them. Immediately they left the boat and their father, and followed him. (Matthew 4:18-22)

Two pairs of brothers are minding their own business by either casting nets or mending them. They are honest laborers taking advantage of the abundant life in the Sea of Galilee, like many others who caught fish, largely for processing and export. The good quality of the fish was well-known even in Rome, where barrels of the pickled fish fetched a good price. As is often the case, the people working to acquire the raw product did not make as much as the merchants who sold it, but it was still a good way of life.

Jesus walks into the scene of fishermen minding their own business, and he takes the initiative to encounter each pair of brothers in order to bestow on them a new, more widespread brotherhood. These brothers are not looking for the opportunity to follow some new rabbi; they are either fishing or getting ready to go fishing. Yet Jesus approaches them.

First, Jesus goes up to the two brothers who have come from Bethsaida, a town on the north end of the lake, near the place where the Jordan River flows into the Sea of Galilee. He invites them to "follow" him and promises to transform them from fishers of fish to "fishers of men" (Matthew 4:19). Though Jesus uses an image based on their own work experience as a model for their new role, it would still have seemed an odd thing to promise. However, it grabs their attention, and they leave their nets and boat to follow him, though they know not where.

The second set of brothers is also approached. They do not respond to the promise made to Simon and Andrew and ask to join Jesus; no, he calls them. They, too, leave their boat and their father, Zebedee, and follow Jesus at his initiative.

Imagine you are going about your business: what would be the activity or behavior that is most typical for you? Then picture Jesus walking up to you and inviting you to "come, follow me." Look at the things around you; what is Jesus inviting you to leave behind in order to follow him? What do you think of that? What is there about Jesus that makes following him so attractive that you are willing to leave your things behind? What might you ask him in regard to following him? What do you fear? What do you look forward to? Speak to him as a friend to a Friend about these issues.

Conclude with Psalm 23.

_____

_____

_____

_____

_____

_____

MEDITATION 4

Preaching, Teaching, and Healing

And he went about all Galilee, teaching in their synagogues and preaching the gospel of the kingdom and healing every disease and every infirmity among the people. So his fame spread throughout all Syria, and they brought him all the sick, those afflicted with various diseases and pains, demoniacs, epileptics, and paralytics, and he healed them. And great crowds followed him from Galilee and the Decapolis and Jerusalem and Judea and from beyond the Jordan. (Matthew 4:23-25)

This summary states that Jesus remained in Galilee, preaching in "their synagogues" (Matthew 4:23) throughout the whole region. The synagogue was the main institution of the Pharisaic party, which was primarily comprised of laypeople who had decided to follow strictly the laws of ritual purity that properly belonged to the priests. The priests mostly belonged to the Sadducean party and were typically neglecting those laws in order to accommodate the prevailing Greek and Roman culture of the time. Within the synagogue, people heard the reading of Scripture every week, using a lectionary cycle whose core was the Torah (the first five books of the Bible), plus readings from the psalms and the prophets. Jesus did not establish a competing institution but taught within the existing Pharisaic synagogues, where he also healed many people.

"His fame spread throughout all Syria" (Matthew 4:24). Syria was the name of the Roman province that encompassed Israel; it was headed by a governor. Within the province were various minor kings, such as Herod Antipas, his brother Philip, and King Aretas in Damascus (2 Corinthians 11:32), as well as the "procurator" Pontius Pilate, an official below governor. Jesus' fame went beyond Galilee to the whole province of Syria, attracting people from every area. (The Decapolis was a group of "ten cities," which is the meaning of *deka polis* in Greek, mostly populated by Gentiles, which are now part of Jordan, including Gerasa [modern Jerash], Philadelphia [modern Amman], Scythopolis, Pella, and others, some of which are mentioned in the Gospels).

Jesus preached, healed, and exorcized all these different people, apparently Jews and Gentiles alike. This passage from Matthew 4 completes the prophecy of Isaiah 9:1-2, which is cited earlier: "The people who sat in darkness have seen a great light, / and for those who sat in the region and shadow of death / light has dawned" (Matthew 4:16). Jesus is a light in the darkness who shines in a variety of ways—preaching, teaching, and healing.

Consider again the contemporary world and its darkness. As you think about the various problems of which you are aware, ask yourself, "In what ways do I want Jesus to shine his light in this world?" What teaching does the contemporary world need to hear from Jesus in order to correct its false assumptions? What preaching would motivate people to believe in Jesus and change their ways?

Where do you want Jesus to bring healing to the parts of the modern world that are hurting and broken? Where does Jesus need to use his power to exorcize demons, and which demons need to be exorcized from the modern world? Who do you know that needs Jesus' healing?

Ask our Lord for the grace of compassion on this world so that you can look upon the world as the Father does. How can you shine in the world, bringing Jesus' light to all who need it? Consider this from the perspective of John 3:16-17: "God so loved the world that he gave his only Son, that whoever believes in him should not perish but have eternal life. For God sent the Son into the world, not to condemn the world, but that the world might be saved through him."

To grow in that loving compassion, pray the Soul of Christ.

_____

_____

_____

_____

_____

_____

_____

_____

_____

_____

_____

_____

_____

_____

_____

_____

CHAPTER 6

The First Exorcism and Manifestation of Jesus' Authority

MARK 1:21-34

Teaching on His Own Authority

And they went into Capernaum; and immediately on the sabbath he entered the synagogue and taught. And they were astonished at his teaching, for he taught them as one who had authority, and not as the scribes. (Mark 1:21-22)

Presumably, the call of Simon Peter, Andrew, John, and James occurred close to Capernaum, since they lived in that small city. Their call took place while they were working, mending and casting their nets, so the Sabbath took place either the next day or a couple of days later. The dark gray basalt stone foundation of that first-century synagogue is still well preserved, though the white limestone walls, pillars, and decorations belong to a late fourth-century synagogue built atop the first-century ruins.

For the first (though hardly the last) time, the people are astonished at the quality of Jesus' teaching. "Scribes" were the more educated members of the Pharisaic party, a lay movement that called for every Jew to live out the ritual and moral purity that the Torah expected of the priests. The priests made up the core of the Sadducean party. However, from the early second century BC, the Sadducean priests and nobles wanted to adapt to the prevailing Greco-Roman culture in clothing styles, cultural expression, and even in the architecture of their homes, as witnessed by the ruins of priests' homes in Jerusalem that employed the same styles of decor as houses in Pompeii (though without Pompeii's idolatry and pornography). A key Pharisaic principle was "putting a fence around Torah," which meant adding various regulations from their oral tradition that prevented a person from breaking God's law. For example, the second commandment prohibits taking the Lord's name in vain; the Pharisees forbade all Jews, except the high priest on the Day of Atonement feast, from ever speaking the Lord's name.

The Pharisees' style of teaching, as evidenced in the Mishna and Talmud, was to list the statements of various rabbis on a particular topic, even if they appeared contradictory. The opinions of different rabbis were cited to show how one position might trump that of another rabbi, and frequently, vigorous debate followed.

Jesus did not teach that way. He did not cite any other rabbis; he did not argue to support the fence around Torah. Rather, he spoke on his own authority. His parables were especially oriented toward explaining his announcement of the nearness of the kingdom of God. His moral teaching went through the commandments to the inner core of the person's heart: "Thou shalt not kill" becomes a commandment against even the anger and revenge that presage killing (Matthew 5:21-26). "Thou shalt not commit adultery" becomes a rejection of lust that initiates immoral actions (5:27-30). Jesus' prohibition of taking oaths is a summons to simply tell the truth at all times, thereby precluding the need for oaths.

Picture yourself sitting on the floor of the synagogue with the majority of congregants. Try to capture the experience of the newness of Jesus' authoritative teaching. Think about the questions that might fill your mind as Jesus asserts "Gospel truth" without mentioning the names of rabbis long familiar to you as sources of authority.

Imagine the questions that begin to formulate in your mind: "do I reject this Jesus of Nazareth as an arrogant man who shows no respect for the traditions of the elders? Or do I let the resonance of true authority with which he speaks lead me to put my faith in him?

Next, consider your own situation. Many claim that new developments in culture and society demand changes in traditional notions of morality. Respect for women means making abortion and contraception available; mercy for the terminally ill means removing their pain by "mercy killing"; acceptance that marriage is too difficult or too limiting means that sex outside of marriage is now normal. Do you accept these modern trends as the inevitable wave of the future, or is the teaching of Jesus Christ more authoritative than the new cultural traditions? Which voice is more authoritative in your mind and heart? Speak to Jesus about the choices you face and listen to what he might tell you.

Conclude with the prayer Soul of Christ.

An Unclean Spirit Is Cast Out

And immediately there was in their synagogue a man with an unclean spirit; and he cried out, "What have you to do with us, Jesus of Nazareth? Have you come to destroy us? I know who you are, the Holy One of God." But Jesus rebuked him, saying, "Be silent, and come out of him!" And the unclean spirit, convulsing him and crying with a loud voice, came out of him. (Mark 1:23-26)

Jesus' authoritative teaching is suddenly disturbed by the presence of a man with an "unclean spirit" who cries out against Jesus and his authority. The unclean spirit's first question assumes that Jesus' presence and teaching are an affront to him and the other demons residing in the man. Apparently, Jesus cannot speak about his kingdom of light without evoking a response from the forces of darkness. (Note the plural "us" used by the spirit here and with the Gerasene demoniac [Mark 5:9]; Jesus teaches about a person who becomes repossessed with seven demons [Matthew 12:45], and he had cast out seven demons from Mary Magdalene [Mark 16:9]).

The key issue is seen in the demons' follow-up question: "Have you come to destroy us?" (Mark 1:24). While the devil's third temptation of Jesus was an offer of the kingdoms of the world on the condition that Jesus would break the first commandment by worshipping him, here the true vulnerability of the evil forces becomes clear: Jesus, who remains ever committed to the core truth of God and proclaims it by his own authority without reference to anyone except his heavenly Father, possesses the infinite goodness of God and therefore he is able to destroy the power of evil. The demons know it and they "shudder" (James 2:19).

Some people, even Christians, fear that evil may be stronger than the good. However, evil is not a positive force of its own but a deprivation of the good through its misuse. For instance, alcohol is a good, and well-regulated consumption of it aids health and may even prolong life; overindulgence is the evil that destroys the liver, impairs reason, weakens the will, and becomes a serious sin. Food is good and necessary, but overindulgence leads to impaired health, obesity, and a neglect of the poor and hungry. Any sin or evil can be examined as a diminishment of the good. We would do well to consider our own behaviors as well as that of others in such a light.

However, this also means that evil derives from that which is good, and therefore the good is both prior in time and in ultimate power. More important, God is the origin of all good, and it is the turning away from God that brings evil. Therefore, his goodness always remains superior to any form of evil. Finally, evil exists in creatures who choose to turn away from God; since they are only creatures and he remains forever the infinite Creator, he will always be infinitely more powerful than the forces of evil.

This leads to the demons' declaration through the possessed man: "I know who you are, the Holy One of God" (Mark 1:24). The demons, who now speak in the singular as "I," recognize the ultimate power that is able to destroy them: the Holy One of God. Though they speak the truth about Jesus, he silences the unclean spirit, which is a general pattern in the Gospels for two reasons. First, Jesus does not accept testimony from the forces of darkness and evil; such a witness can never be trusted. Second, the one time that Jesus does not silence a person who correctly identifies him as the "Son of God" is the centurion's declaration when Jesus dies on the cross (Matthew 27:54). This indicates that the most authentic circumstance for identifying Jesus is not in the context of exorcizing or healing people but in the moment of his redeeming death—the death of God made man for the forgiveness of sins and the ultimate defeat of evil and death itself.

Again, imagine yourself in the same synagogue, seated on the floor, amazed at Jesus' teaching. You are trying to sort out your thoughts about his authoritative teaching when a demonic voice yells at Jesus. Feel the shock at the sound of the voice. How do you react to that accusatory voice? How do you react to Jesus' response and his power to silence and drive out the demon?

Next, consider where you see Satan most active today. How do you want to respond? Speak to Jesus about how best to bring his love and peace to the situation in order to replace the evil that you perceive.

Finally, ask him for the gift of faith to believe that your prayer, in his name, will dispel the evil. Ask him for the grace to persist in prayer so that you can continue to pray against the evil spirits you see working in the world today.

Conclude with the prayer Soul of Christ.

The Congregation Reacts to the Exorcism

And they were all amazed, so that they questioned among themselves, saying, "What is this? A new teaching! With authority he commands even the unclean spirits, and they obey him." And at once his fame spread everywhere throughout all the surrounding region of Galilee. (Mark 1:27-28)

Jesus' power to exorcize the demons by the authority of his spoken word now confirms the authority of his new teaching about the kingdom of God. His authority to forgive sins by his word will later be confirmed by his healing of the paralytic (Mark 2:1-12). The congregation's reaction of being "amazed" (1:27) is as strong as their "astonished" reaction in Mark 1:22, and is followed by the question "What is this?" They piece together an answer with statements about "a new teaching" and "authority" over unclean spirits (1:27), but these are merely "dots" of data that they are presently unable to connect to provide a complete picture of Jesus. Their question is quite important, and the rest of the Gospel will be needed to connect the other dots of data so as to form a fuller picture of the reality of Jesus Christ.

Picture yourself among the other congregants in the synagogue. What would you say to them in the discussion about Jesus? What bits of knowledge about Jesus do you fix upon in order to form your opinion of him at this stage of the discussion of his ministry?

Then consider your life today. What elements of the Gospel presentation of Jesus form the highlights of your decision to be a Christian? How do you analyze and evaluate these things that you know about him? What still amazes you about Jesus? What questions do you still have about him? Picture him there with you, just as he was in the synagogue with the now exorcized man, and pose your questions to him. Tell him what still amazes and even perplexes you about him. What might he say about these things at this stage of your life of faith?

Conclude with the prayer Soul of Christ.

_____

_____

_____

_____

_____

_____

_____

_____

_____

_____

_____

_____

_____

_____

_____

_____

_____

Jesus Heals Simon Peter's Mother-in-Law

And immediately he left the synagogue, and entered the house of Simon and Andrew, with James and John. Now Simon's mother-in-law lay sick with a fever, and immediately they told him of her. And he came and took her by the hand and lifted her up, and the fever left her; and she served them. (Mark 1:29-31)

The house of Simon and Andrew in Capernaum is only about forty yards from the synagogue. Its ruins can still be seen, along with a second-century "house church" and a fourth-century octagonal church built over the original house. Peter's name is scratched into the ancient stone, and archeologists have found two first-century fish hooks in between the basalt paving stones of the ancient floor. A modern chapel, shaped like an abstract boat, is built on stilts above the ruins, with a clear plastic floor in the center so that visitors can see the ancient structures and consider this scene of the healing of Peter's mother-in-law as well as the healing of the paralytic let down through the roof (Mark 2:1-12).

Simon's mother-in-law is sick, and Jesus heals her by merely taking her hand. After her healing, she immediately turns to the needs of others and serves them, so she becomes something of an ideal for any person who experiences Jesus' healing touch. Jesus' healing is not merely some form of inexpensive health care but an enabling to look beyond oneself to the needs of other people.

Imagine that you are Peter's mother-in-law. What is your reaction to being freed of the fever? Can you recall a time when you had a fever and it finally broke? How did you feel at that point? Did weakness and fatigue remain afterward? Did you feel completely recovered yet?

In light of your own experience of overcoming a high fever, consider the healed woman getting up immediately to serve Jesus and the disciples. Another quality of healing occurred for her that was beyond the natural process of the body healing itself. She possessed a strength that is absent when someone is healed by medicine or when the illness has run it natural course. Jesus' healing empowered her, and she used that new strength in service of others.

Now consider your own life. Have any of your encounters with Jesus been a source of healing for you—physically, emotionally, or spiritually? After having received the healing, what did you do? Have you found ways in which that healing made you more sensitive to other people in the same condition? Have your encounters with Jesus led you to greater service?

Having recalled some of these experiences of your own, now have a conversation with Jesus about them. What does he want you to do with the healings you have received? Have you done what he desired? Have you respond to him with generosity, or have you taken the healing for granted? Ask him what he expects of you now.

Conclude with an Our Father.

_____

_____

_____

MEDITATION 5

Jesus Heals and Exorcizes
After the Sabbath Is Over

That evening, at sundown, they brought to him all who were
sick or possessed with demons. And the whole city was gath-
ered together about the door. And he healed many who were
sick with various diseases, and cast out many demons; and he
would not permit the demons to speak, because they knew him.
(Mark 1:32-34)

S undown marks the end of the Sabbath, in Jesus' day and
today. The Pharisees had various regulations for the Sabbath that were intended to protect its holiness. Therefore
the townspeople waited until sundown—marked by the point
at which they could see three stars in the evening sky—to carry
their sick and demon-possessed to Jesus. The congregation had
witnessed the exorcism in the synagogue and they would have
heard of the healing of Peter's mother-in-law, since such news
spread easily in a small city like Capernaum where the houses
were crowded close to one another. They could barely wait for
the Sabbath to be over, and the whole area around the door
of Simon Peter's house was overflowing with those in need of
Jesus' healing.

This passage, a summary of Jesus' ministry against diseases
and demons, indicates the extent of the power of the kingdom
of darkness in the lives of common people. Jesus responds with
this announcement: "The time is fulfilled, and the kingdom of
God is at hand; repent, and believe in the gospel" (Mark 1:15),

as had John the Baptist. However, he does more: he overcomes the devil's temptations in the wilderness (Mark 1:13,) and he engages the kingdom of darkness in direct combat.

Picture yourself observing this scene in front of Peter's house as Jesus heals illnesses and casts out demons, not by blaming the afflicted for their problems, but by commanding healing and freedom from the forces of evil. During this combat, he again silences the demons who announce what they know of him. He refuses to accept their identification of him; he simply demonstrates his authority to command them and drive them out, proving that truly "the time is fulfilled, and the kingdom of God is at hand."

Now consider the long history of pain and evil in the world and the ways in which Jesus has continued to heal people. Think about the hospitals, mental institutions, and medical schools founded by Catholic monks, nuns, religious, and laity, who have often also staffed many of those establishments through the centuries. Think of the ways that the Lord has sent people like Blessed Mother Teresa of Calcutta and her brothers, sisters, and volunteers to serve Jesus in the poorest of the poor. Think of the many religious and lay groups that have been founded to relieve suffering; some have ministered to and even liberated the enslaved or have served refugees from violence and war. Many other groups who suffer continue today to be served by Jesus Christ and his Church.

As you consider these realities, speak to Jesus about what he is asking of you. What are the sufferings and evils that you see around you today? Who belongs to the crowd that would gather at the door of Peter's house if they realized that Jesus was inside to heal them? To which of these suffering people do you feel drawn to help? What is the reason or basis of that attraction?

Ask Jesus for the wisdom to know what he wants you to do in today's world and for the grace of the Holy Spirit to empower you to do it.

Conclude with the prayer Soul of Christ.

_____

_____

_____

_____

_____

_____

_____

_____

_____

_____

_____

_____

_____

_____

_____

_____

_____

_____

_____

_____

_____

_____

_____

_____

_____

_____

_____

_____

_____

_____

_____

_____

_____

_____

_____

_____

_____

_____

_____

_____

_____

_____

_____

_____

_____

_____

CHAPTER 7

The Transition from Capernaum to the Galilean Mission

MARK 1:35-39

Jesus Sets Out Alone to Pray

And in the morning, a great while before day, he rose and went out to a lonely place, and there he prayed. (Mark 1:35)

This verse, so early in Jesus' public ministry, gives the first of many examples of personal private prayer in his life (the parallel version is Luke 4:42). He goes off early in the day, before anyone else is awake to notice him, to a lonely place for prayerful communion with his Father. According to early Jewish-Christian tradition, Jesus often prayed at a small grotto on the southeastern side of the Mount of Beatitudes, just across from Tabgha, the modern name for the area where he multiplied the loaves and fishes.

The Gospels, and those of St. Mark and St. Luke in particular, take note of Jesus going off for private prayer:

After the multiplication of loaves—Mark 6:46: And after he had taken leave of them, he went up on the mountain to pray.

Immediately before choosing his twelve apostles—Luke 6:12: In these days he went into the hills to pray; and all night he continued in prayer to God.

Before Peter's profession of faith that Jesus is the Christ—Luke 9:18: Now it happened that as he was praying alone the disciples were with him; and he asked them, "Who do the people say that I am?"

Immediately before the Transfiguration—Luke 9:28: Now about eight days after these sayings he took with him Peter and John and James, and went up on the mountain to pray.

Before teaching the Our Father—Luke 11:1: He was praying in a certain place, and when he ceased, one of his disciples said to him, "Lord, teach us to pray, as John taught his disciples."

Before the crucifixion in the Garden of Gethsemane—Matthew 26:36-45; Mark 14:32-41; Luke 22:39-46.

Coming from his own experience of private personal prayer, Jesus teaches his disciples to do the same:

> "And when you pray, you must not be like the hypocrites; for they love to stand and pray in the synagogues and at the street corners, that they may be seen by men. Truly, I say to you, they have received their reward. But when you pray, go into your room and shut the door and pray to your Father who is in secret; and your Father who sees in secret will reward you." (Matthew 6:5-6)

Such prayer of communion with God provides important spiritual sustenance to living out the Christian pilgrimage. Within such private prayer, one can gain a sensitivity to the movements of the Holy Spirit, thereby becoming alert to the ways in which God is leading one to a particular vocation, apostolate, or other task.

Imagine that as Jesus went out to pray by himself, he quietly invited you to join him in his secret place. Try to picture Jesus at prayer. Where would his attention be? What would be the expression on his face? What would his posture be? Quietly remain with him.

Then, when he finishes, imagine yourself in a conversation with Jesus about your own prayer life. Speak to him about the way in which you presently pray. Then ask him what he would look for from you. What is his goal for your private prayer? What more would he desire from you in this area of your life? How do you respond to him?

Jesus taught the Our Father immediately after an occasion of private prayer (Luke 11:1-4) and after his instruction for his disciples to pray alone (Matthew 6:5-13). Conclude this meditation with the Our Father, praying it along with Jesus.

_____

_____

_____

_____

_____

_____

_____

_____

_____

_____

_____

_____

_____

_____

_____

What Does Jesus Seek in His Prayer?

And in the morning, a great while before day, he rose and went
out to a lonely place, and there he prayed. (Mark 1:35)

We would do well to repeat our meditation on this verse, this time by considering not only the fact that Jesus prayed privately but also his desire to enter into communion with his Father and seek his will. Jesus emptied himself of the glory of heaven and did not cling to his divinity:

> Have this mind among yourselves, which was in Christ Jesus, who, though he was in the form of God, did not count equality with God a thing to be grasped, but emptied himself, taking the form of a servant, being born in the likeness of men. And being found in human form he humbled himself and became obedient unto death, even death on a cross. (Philippians 2:5-8)

From this humble mind-set, Jesus seeks to know the Father's will step-by-step. By seeking the Father's will in this way, he constantly stays in communication with the Father. This shows not only the importance of doing what the Father wills, but also the importance of his ongoing relationship with the Father. Neither aspect can be neglected.

No Gospel emphasizes the importance of Jesus doing the will of the Father who sent him as much as the Gospel of John. Consider the following verses, which are just a few that treat this aspect of Jesus' self-understanding:

"My food is to do the will of him who sent me, and to accomplish his work." (4:34)

"Truly, truly, I say to you, the Son can do nothing of his own accord, but only what he sees the Father doing; for whatever he does, that the Son does likewise." (5:19)

"I can do nothing on my own authority; as I hear, I judge; and my judgment is just, because I seek not my own will but the will of him who sent me." (5:30)

"For I have come down from heaven, not to do my own will, but the will of him who sent me." (6:38)

"I do nothing on my own authority but speak thus as the Father taught me." (8:28)

"We must work the works of him who sent me, while it is day." (9:4)

"For I have not spoken on my own authority; the Father who sent me has himself given me commandment what to say and what to speak. And I know that his commandment is eternal life. What I say, therefore, I say as the Father has bidden me." (12:49-50)

Jesus also speaks to the Father at the Last Supper in his prayer in John 17, emphasizing that he has sought only to do the Father's will:

"I glorified thee on earth, having accomplished the work which thou gavest me to do." (17:4)

"I have given them the words which thou gavest me." (17:8)

In these passages, Jesus teaches us by his example that our time of prayer is not only for asking the Father for the things we need (which is still, of course, a very important aspect of the prayer that Jesus teaches in the Our Father), but also for turning to the Father in prayer to discover his will for us.

What is the mission that God has for me? What is the next stage of that mission? Where does the Lord want me to go next? We can each pray that we will be as faithful to our own vocation as Jesus is to his.

Again, imagine yourself in the small grotto praying with Jesus. Consider how he enters deeply into communion with his heavenly Father. Ask the Father, in the name of Jesus Christ, for the gift of the Holy Spirit to help you enter more deeply into communion with him. As St. Paul wrote, "The Spirit helps us in our weakness; for we do not know how to pray as we ought" (Romans 8:26).

Next, ask the Father for the grace to know his will in your life and to desire to do it. Repeat some of the quotes from John's Gospel listed here. One at a time, consider slowly and prayerfully how you can say those same words of Jesus with meaning and integrity. Mull over each verse, considering whether your food is to do the will of the Father and whether your words are those that the Father wants you to speak. Pray that you receive the Holy Spirit to enable you to think like Jesus, conform your will like Jesus, and act and live like Jesus.

Conclude with an Our Father, especially concentrating on the first petitions.

_____

_____

_____

_____

_____

_____

_____

_____

_____

_____

_____

_____

_____

_____

_____

_____

_____

_____

_____

_____

_____

The Next Stage of Jesus' Ministry

And Simon and those who were with him followed him, and they found him and said to him, "Every one is searching for you." And he said to them, "Let us go on to the next towns, that I may preach there also; for that is why I came out." And he went throughout all Galilee, preaching in their synagogues and casting out demons. (Mark 1:36-39)

Simon Peter has no comprehension of the importance of Jesus' private prayer; he can only focus on the multitude of people who are seeking Jesus for more healings, exorcisms, and teachings. One gets the sense that Simon simply wants to keep Jesus at his home so that everyone will continue coming there, thus keeping the attention on Jesus in Capernaum.

Jesus does not seek to please Simon or to conform to Simon's desires. Rather, Jesus knows that he must set out to accomplish the task for which he came. The goal of his mission was to come to earth and to the whole people of Israel to whom the Lord had promised a new covenant (Jeremiah 31:31), and not just to Capernaum. He informs Simon, therefore, that he must go "to the next towns" (Mark 1:38) and preach to them about the coming of the kingdom of God and the consequent need for repentance and faith in order to enter it. Simon must decide at this point whether he wants to tie down Jesus to an already successful mission in Capernaum or follow him on the mission "to the next towns."

Imagine yourself as Simon, seeking Jesus all over the town of Capernaum and then looking outside town, taking wrong directions, walking up the hill now known as the Mount of Beatitudes, and finally coming upon Jesus in the cave after a number of hours of persistent searching.

Then consider the way in which your thoughts would need to adjust themselves, from a desire for yet more success locally to a decision to follow Jesus into unknown situations. How much trust are you willing to place in Jesus at this point? Speak to Jesus about your ability to trust his leadership in taking the next step of the mission to which he has invited you. Examine your willingness to take on new risks with him. What does this stir within you? Speak to him about this as a friend to a Friend.

Conclude with the prayer Soul of Christ.

Put Out into the Deep

LUKE 5:1-11

Jesus Teaches a Crowd from Simon's Boat

While the people pressed upon him to hear the word of God, he was standing by the lake of Gennesaret. And he saw two boats by the lake; but the fishermen had gone out of them and were washing their nets. Getting into one of the boats, which was Simon's, he asked him to put out a little from the land. And he sat down and taught the people from the boat. (Luke 5:1-3)

S t. Luke presents an important episode with Simon Peter and his partners that takes place after Jesus sets forth from Capernaum. Jesus is preaching to crowds at the Lake of Gennesaret, elsewhere in the Gospels known as the Sea of Galilee, or, in John's Gospel, as the Sea of Tiberias (6:1; 21:1). Hebrew and other Semitic languages use the word "sea" for any large body of water, while the Greeks, who were very capable seafarers, distinguished terms such as "sea" from "lake." The name "Gennesaret" comes from the Gennesar plain on the northwest shore of the lake, between Magdala and Capernaum. The Hebrew and Aramaic word *ge* means "valley," while the root *nsr* gives the meaning of an "enclosed valley," a good name for this very fertile region.

As part of Jesus' ministry near his new home in Capernaum, he stands at the lakeshore teaching. Just south of Capernaum is a cove known as "the cove of the parables," from a tradition that Jesus frequently taught there. It forms a natural amphitheater and is a good location for people to sit and listen to someone speaking. However, Jesus experiences difficulties because the crowds press upon him, apparently pushing to get close to this teacher. To make for a more relaxed experience of teaching, he climbs into a boat and asks Simon to put it out a little from the shore so that he can teach. The water also amplifies his voice, enabling the people to hear him more easily.

Jesus had stated in Mark 1:38 that to "preach" was "why I came." In this scene, Jesus is not interested in receiving adulation from the crowd but in giving them the truth of the word he has received from his Father. Therefore, he gets into Peter's boat so that he can better teach them.

Consider the modern temptation to keep ourselves in the public eye, which is especially possible today with the advent of social media. For many, it is integral to their careers to make appearances at a variety of public events and to keep the Internet buzzing with their names and activities. Some even cite the modern proverb that there is no such thing as bad publicity. Even if we are not interested in climbing the career ladder, we often want others to notice us or give us attention.

Then turn to Jesus, who is not interested in receiving attention from the crowd but in teaching and preaching. He is more interested in others than in himself. He is more interested in doing the Father's will than in bringing attention to himself.

What about you? Do you ever fantasize about being famous or even just being the center of attention? Do you say or do things just to draw attention to yourself? Or do you seek to serve the people around you, without focusing on yourself? Are your personal needs more important, or are theirs? This is an example of the basic kind of choice that we make in following Jesus:

do we really want the world's version of fame or Jesus' version of service?

Speak to Jesus and examine your motives in this regard. Let him search your inner heart and your deeper motivations and needs. Then make the decision to be like him.

Conclude with the prayer Soul of Christ.

_____

_____

_____

_____

_____

_____

_____

_____

_____

_____

_____

_____

_____

_____

_____

_____

_____

_____

Jesus Rewards Simon with a Catch of Fish

And when he had ceased speaking, he said to Simon, "Put out into the deep and let down your nets for a catch." And Simon answered, "Master, we toiled all night and took nothing! But at your word I will let down the nets." And when they had done this, they enclosed a great shoal of fish; and as their nets were breaking, they beckoned to their partners in the other boat to come and help them. And they came and filled both the boats, so that they began to sink. (Luke 5:4-7)

The content of Jesus' words to the people is left out by St. Luke in order to emphasize the effect of Jesus' next word to Simon and his partners. Jesus, the carpenter from Nazareth, gives Simon, the fisherman from Bethsaida (meaning "house of fishing"), an order to go to the deep area of the lake. (The surface of the lake is 683 feet below sea level, and another 126 feet lower at its deepest point.) Simon, the professional fisherman, responds to the carpenter that he and his partners have been at work all night—the normal time for fishing because the fish cannot see the nets coming over them—and yet they have caught nothing. In fact, the afternoon was better suited to a good long nap before returning to work that night. Nonetheless, despite knowing better, Simon agrees to let down his nets at the Master's word.

The result of obeying Jesus' word was a catch so abundant that the nets began to break and the boat began to sink from the weight of the fish. The abundance even spread to the boat of Simon's partners.

Consider Jesus' order to Simon, and think back on a time when either the words of Scripture or some personal inspiration in prayer seemed to be telling you to do something apparently absurd. Like Simon, you knew the situation well, and you had plenty of experience to back up your reluctance. Your human experience was not to be lightly disregarded. Yet the idea persisted, and you felt drawn in some mysterious way to follow the sense of peace that came with the idea of obeying the words of the Bible or the inspiration you felt.

Imagine yourself as Simon, his brother Andrew, or their partners James and John. As the largest catch of fish in your life unfolds before you, what comes to your mind? What might you feel as, first, you are proven wrong about fishing in broad daylight? Then, how do you feel as the catch becomes abundant? Finally, as the number of fish brings your boat to the point of sinking, what crosses your mind about Jesus?

Finally, consider those times when you made a decision to trust Jesus with a big decision, such as marriage, a vocation to the religious life or the priesthood, or some other major issue. If you have seen it unfold in a way better than you could have imagined, what is your attitude toward Jesus? Speak to him about how it is working out and about what he might expect you to do next.

Conclude with the prayer Soul of Christ.

_____

_____

_____

The Decisive Exchange between Simon Peter and Jesus

But when Simon Peter saw it, he fell down at Jesus' knees, saying, "Depart from me, for I am a sinful man, O Lord." For he was astonished, and all that were with him, at the catch of fish which they had taken; and so also were James and John, sons of Zebedee, who were partners with Simon. And Jesus said to Simon, "Do not be afraid; henceforth you will be catching men." (Luke 5:8-10)

S imon is designated for the first time as "Simon Peter" (Luke 5:8), pointing to the new name and identity that Jesus will bestow upon him later in the Gospel at Caesarea Philippi. Already, Simon Peter's willingness to repent shows itself. He recognizes the great catch as a miracle of which he is unworthy because he is a "sinful man." This is not the confession of a person who has been far distant from God; in fact, later in Acts 10:14, Luke records Peter's statement that he had never eaten any "common or unclean" food in his life, indicating that he had always been an observant Jew.

A better understanding of his self-identification as a "sinful man" comes from such great saints as Paul, Francis of Assisi, Ignatius of Loyola, and others, who saw themselves as the worst of sinners. This is not some tradition of false humility but an indication of the saints' closeness to God. The farther a person is from God, the more willing he or she is to accept sinful behavior as normal; the closer one comes to God, the more his saving light makes a person's sinfulness visible. Holy people are better able to contrast their behavior with the holiness of God only because they are more alert to his goodness. Those immersed in sin tend to compare themselves to other sinners and derive a certain amount of comfort from being no worse than the people around them.

Here, Simon Peter realizes through the miracle that he is in the presence of the Holy One, and he is afraid of Jesus' presence. As the great catch of fish shows, Jesus' holiness is far more powerful than Simon's expertise as a lifelong fisherman. Yet it is to this humble fisherman that Jesus speaks a phrase well known throughout the Bible when angels or God himself appears to people: "Be not afraid" (see Isaiah 41:10; 14; 43:1; 44:2; Matthew 28:5; Luke 1:13, 30; 12:32; Acts 18:9-10; 27:24). This command not to be afraid is followed by a call: "I will make you fishers of men" (as in Matthew 4:19; cf. Mark 1:17).

Imagine yourself as Simon Peter observing this miracle of the great catch, and try to enter into his fear at being in the presence of someone who can teach so profoundly and even change some of the ways of nature.

Then consider both Jesus' words of comfort—"Do not be afraid"—and his challenge: "Henceforth you will be catching men" (Luke 5:10). In what ways have you experienced Jesus extending comfort to you when you were frightened by him or by the challenges of your life? Have some particular passages of Scripture been a source of comfort? How would you speak to Jesus about that command to let go of fear?

Jesus challenges Simon and his partners from within their own experience as fishermen: "I will make you fishers of men" (Matthew 4:19). Jesus does not reject their past experience but builds upon it. In what ways has Jesus used you, with your own past abilities and experiences, to enter into his mission? Make an offering of all that you are and give it to the Lord for his disposal, for his mission to the world.

Conclude with the Suscipe (Appendix).

_____

_____

_____

_____

_____

_____

_____

_____

_____

_____

_____

_____

_____

_____

_____

_____

_____

_____

_____

_____

_____

MEDITATION 4

The First Disciples Leave
Everything and Follow Jesus

*And when they had brought their boats to land, they left
everything and followed him. (Luke 5:11)*

The first disciples left everything—including the greatest
catch of fish in their career—and followed Jesus, thereby
accepting his new vocation as "fishers of men." They
were not yet filled with all the courage they would eventually
need, as will be seen in Gethsemane and in the court of the
high priest Caiaphas. Nor were they fully committed to leaving
behind their boats and nets, as in John 21, where Peter leads the
other disciples to go fishing. Their conversion, depth of faith,
and understanding would take time and many experiences with
Jesus over his three-year period of public ministry.

However, after Jesus' resurrection and ascension into heaven
and the Holy Spirit's descent on Pentecost, the disciples would
cast their nets into the depths of Jerusalem, Judea, Samaria, and
even to the ends of the world, as Jesus had instructed them (Acts
1:8). Through them, the world would come to know of Jesus.
Through their ministry in the first century, the grace of God
would change countless hearts.

During the Jubilee Year in 2000, St. John Paul II made much
of Jesus' order to "put out into the deep" (Luke 5:4). St. Peter
was told to row farther out into the lake; John Paul saw this as
a symbol of the modern world, into whose depths each Christian is to let down his or her nets to catch many souls for Jesus

Christ. Each of us can say, "Leave me, Lord, for I am a sinner," and each of us can hear Jesus' call to become "fishers of men" (cf. Luke 5:8, 10).

Imagine yourself as Simon and his partners leaving their boats, nets, and other equipment to follow Jesus. What would be the stronger pull for you: reluctance and fear of leaving behind your possessions and way of life or joy at following Jesus into his mission?

What do you think the Lord Jesus might be asking you to leave behind in order to follow him? What has he already asked you to leave behind in order to follow him? What is your attitude toward that? Do you find yourself apprehensive or fearful? Will you respond like Simon Peter, Andrew, James, and John? Picture Jesus as he stands before you, waiting for your response: What do you say to him?

Conclude with the Suscipe.

_____

_____

_____

_____

_____

_____

_____

_____

_____

_____

Appendix of Prayers

Soul of Christ

Soul of Christ, sanctify me.
Body of Christ, save me.
Blood of Christ, inebriate me.
Water from the side of Christ, wash me.
Passion of Christ, strengthen me.
O good Jesus, hear me.
Within your wounds, hide me.
Let me never be separated from you.
From the wicked foe, defend me.
At the hour of my death call me and bid me come to you
So that with your angels and saints I may praise you
For all eternity.

Come, Holy Spirit

Come, Holy Spirit, fill the hearts of your faithful, and kindle
in them the fire of your love.
V: Send forth your Spirit, and they shall be created.
R: And you shall renew the face of the earth.

Let us pray:
O God, who did teach the hearts of your faithful people by
sending them the light of your Holy Spirit, grant us by the same
Spirit to have a right judgment in all things, and evermore to
rejoice in his holy comfort. Through Christ our Lord. Amen.

The Suscipe

Take, Lord, receive my liberty, my understanding, my memory, my entire will.

You have given me all that I have and possess, and I return it all to you, Lord.

Everything is yours; do with it what you will.

Give me only your love and your grace, that is enough for me.

the WORD among us ®
The Spirit of Catholic Living

T his book was published by The Word Among Us. Since 1981, The Word Among Us has been answering the call of the Second Vatican Council to help Catholic laypeople encounter Christ in the Scriptures.

The name of our company comes from the prologue to the Gospel of John and reflects the vision and purpose of all of our publications: to be an instrument of the Spirit, whose desire is to manifest Jesus' presence in and to the children of God. In this way, we hope to contribute to the Church's ongoing mission of proclaiming the gospel to the world so that all people would know the love and mercy of our Lord and grow ever more deeply in love with him.

Our monthly devotional magazine, *The Word Among Us*, features meditations on the daily and Sunday Mass readings, and currently reaches more than one million Catholics in North America and another half million Catholics in one hundred countries around the world. Our book division, The Word Among Us Press, publishes numerous books, Bible studies, and pamphlets that help Catholics grow in their faith.

To learn more about who we are and what we publish, log on to our website at www.wau.org. There you will find a variety of Catholic resources that will help you grow in your faith.

Embrace His Word, Listen to God . . .

www.wau.org